A FIELD GUIDE TO

AUSTRALIAN
TREES

A FIELD GUIDE TO

AUSTRALIAN TREES

IVAN HOLLIDAY

LANSDOWNE

Published by Lansdowne Publishing Pty Ltd
Level 5, 70 George Street, Sydney NSW 2000, Australia

First published by Rigby Publishers 1969
Reprinted 1971, 1972
Revised (colour) edition 1974
Reprinted 1975, 1976, 1979, 1983, 1984, 1986, 1987

Second revised edition published in 1989 by
Hamlyn Australia
a division of the Octopus Publishing Group
Reprinted by Lansdowne Publishing 1994

Edited by Tony Bishop
Designed by Sue Burk
Typeset in Australia by Savage Type Pty Ltd, Brisbane
Printed in Singapore by Kyodo Shing Loong Printing Pte Ltd.

National Library of Australia Cataloguing-in-Publication Data

Holliday, Ivan, 1926–
A field guide to Australian trees.

ISBN 1 86302 395 X

1. Trees — Australia — Identification. I. Title
582.160994

CONTENTS

Eucalyptus grandis

Introduction

This field guide was originally published in 1969, when my very good friend, the late Ron Hill, assisted in its preparation by providing the line drawings. Over the years, these illustrations have been an essential component of the book to assist the reader in identifying a particular tree.

Consequently, in compiling this new edition, many of Ron's original sketches have been reincluded (with kind permission from his sister, Barbara), where they are still appropriate. These will serve as a reminder of one of Ron's many talents.

The text has, however, been completely revised to include all taxonomic changes which have occurred recently, as well as other information worthy of inclusion. Many of the photographs have also been replaced, hopefully with improvements. Furthermore, descriptions, photographs and sketches of forty-four additional species have been included.

The book is essentially one for the ordinary person: to assist them to recognise Australian trees which they may encounter throughout all environments of this vast continent.

When one realises, however, that over 500 *Eucalyptus* species are endemic to this country, and that one square kilometre of Queensland rainforest may include over 100 different species, it becomes obvious that many trees must be omitted in a book like this.

An attempt has been made to cover representative species from all of the more common genera, as well as the wide-ranging habitats from arid to rainforest and from subalpine to tropical. It is hoped that it will stimulate interest in the travelling Australian and in the overseas visitor to identify and appreciate the beauty of the trees of Australia.

WALLANGARRA WATTLE

Acacia adunca A. Cunn. ex G. Don
MIMOSACEAE

Wallangarra Wattle is found over a relatively restricted area of the tablelands near the New South Wales–Queensland border. It is better known, however, in cultivation, and is grown extensively in New Zealand, where it is known as Golden Glory.

The genus *Acacia* comprises over 700 recorded species, most being endemic to Australia. These range from trees and shrubs of all sizes to prostrate ground cover plants.

Like many of the wattles, as they are known in Australia, the tree loses its true compound leaves (feathery or bipinnate) as it develops to maturity. They are replaced by phyllodes, which are really flattened leaf stalks. Phyllodes appear in many shapes and sizes on different species of *Acacia*, from small and rounded to long and narrow, or needle-like, and look exactly like simple, true leaves.

This tree is only small — seldom more than 7 m high — and usually erect, with narrow graceful foliage. Phyllodes are long and very narrow, dark shiny green in colour, and the young shoots are silky. The feathery true leaves persist for some time on young trees and return when the tree is cut. Bark is smooth and light grey.

It flowers in early spring (in autumn in Queensland) producing masses of globular yellow inflorescences in showy terminal clusters; this feature is well illustrated in the photograph opposite. All species of *Acacia* have either these ball-shaped (globular) inflorescences, or rod-shaped ones (cylindrical spikes); they consist largely of numerous, closely compacted stamens, varying in colour from cream to a deep orange-yellow.

Acacia seeds, contained in small bean-like pods, are black and shiny and have a very hard outer covering (testa) which keeps the seed viable for a long period of time.

This is an ornamental tree that is spectacular in flower; it is suitable for cultivating in areas of moderate rainfall. It prefers well-drained, non-limy soils, but is adaptable.

BOWER LEAF WATTLE *A. cognata* Domin. Another lovely tree to 12 m high with narrow phyllodes. Although its flowers are unspectacular, the species stands out because of its beautiful foliage which gives the tree the look of a soft, wispy green cloud drooping to ground level among its harder-foliaged companions. It is found in wet forest areas of eastern Victoria and in southern New South Wales near the coast. This species has been confused with the broader-foliaged *Acacia subporosa* F. Muell.

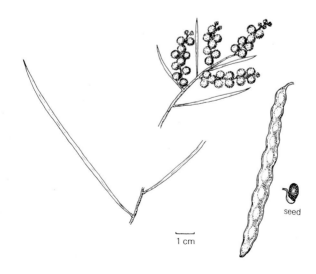

1 cm

seed

MULGA

Acacia aneura F. Muell. ex Benth.

MIMOSACEAE

Mulga is a tree of the arid inland. It is found over an extensive range in all States except Victoria and Tasmania.

The term 'mulga' is one frequently used by Australians when referring to any piece of scrubland, although, in fact, true Mulga scrub is not seen near any of the major cities.

In the wetter parts of its habitat range, Mulga sometimes occurs in dense thickets that are hard to penetrate; elsewhere it is often scattered throughout open country. Soils can be red sand dunes, stony or rocky, or, more usually, heavy clays subjected to flooding after heavy rains which often do not fall for several years at a time.

The tree is only small, 5 m or less, to 10 m in height at its best, with an umbrella-like crown, but extremely variable in both habit and foliage. The foliage is usually silvery grey, and the inflorescences are deep yellow and rod-shaped. Flowering time is variable according to rainfall.

Phyllodes are variable, sometimes almost round, but often long and narrow, curved or straight. The seed pods are glabrous, broad, and flat, 1–4 cm long.

Mulga wood is well known for its use in the ornamental souvenir trade where it is cut and highly polished to show its characteristic hard dark brown and yellow grain.

For many centuries the Mulga has survived the harsh drought-stricken areas of inland Australia, often where human and beast are unable to survive. Like other trees of the same arid regions, Mulga is a very necessary part of nature's balance. It is an excellent fodder tree, and, over the years, the running of stock in these parts has had a marked effect on tree life.

Mulga is long-lived and well worth cultivating in dry areas. The extra watering given to cultivated trees produces more regular flowering.

UMBRELLA MULGA *A. brachystachya* Benth. is a very similar small tree to 7 m, but always has narrow phyllodes. The seed pods are different from those of *A. aneura*, being woody and covered with fine hairs.

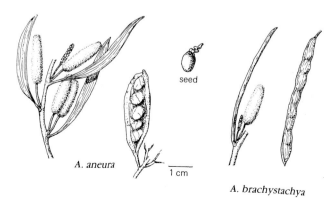

A. aneura   seed

┌─────┐
 1 cm

A. brachystachya

COOTAMUNDRA WATTLE

Acacia baileyana F. Muell.
MIMOSACEAE

An original inhabitant of a very limited area of southern New South Wales in the Cootamundra and Wagga districts, Cootamundra Wattle is probably the most commonly cultivated of all the wattle trees — in Australia, at least.

Because of its lovely silvery blue foliage it is often called Silver Wattle, although another species, *A. dealbata*, has been assigned this common name. Seldom, if ever, seen in its original habitat, the tree has sometimes regenerated so well elsewhere from planted specimens that it could almost be considered a native of these areas.

This is a very beautiful species for the first 10–15 years of its rather short life span. It grows rapidly and is pyramidal in the early stages with branches to ground level, but it later develops a dense, rounded crown supported by a short trunk. Leaves are small and feathery, composed of numerous finely divided pinnae at right angles to the leaf stalk, and a mealy blue in colour. The smaller branches, too, are glaucous, and the trunk and main branches persist in this same colouring for a number of years, but later turn grey as they age.

In flower it is spectacular, simply loaded down in midwinter by numerous trusses of small, fluffy yellow flower balls. Unfortunately they are sometimes spoilt by rain.

The tree's relatively short life can, to some extent, be prolonged by judicious pruning each year after flowering, to promote vigorous new growth.

In spite of these drawbacks this is a beautiful species, both for foliage and for flowers, and has proved its popularity over the years. It is best planted in moist, acid soils in cool, hilly locations, where it can be allowed to regenerate naturally among other trees, particularly on the large estates, although it is adaptable and easily grown in other situations.

QUEENSLAND SILVER WATTLE or **MT MORGAN WATTLE** *A. podalyriifolia* A. Cunn. is another often cultivated tree with lovely mealy blue foliage. This species, however, belongs to the group with phyllodes, these being broad and rounded on this particular tree. It is long-flowering from May to July, is not unduly rain-spoilt and is a lovely sight in full bloom. This is a very beautiful species, best suited to non-limy soils.

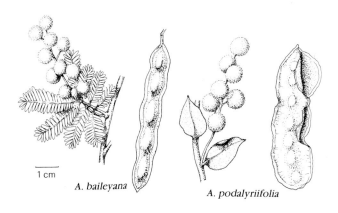

A. baileyana   *A. podalyriifolia*

1 cm

GIDGEE, STINKING WATTLE

Acacia cambagei R. T. Baker
MIMOSACEAE

Gidgee is native to the dry areas of inland temperate Australia, but does not extend into Western Australia. Where it occurs it is often the dominant tree, particularly when found along watercourses and in clay depressions where water collects after rain. Under these conditions it forms pure stands of dense scrub with interlacing branches, often bordering the treeless gibber plains.

At its best it forms a handsome and dense tree up to 10 m in height, with a wide-spreading, drooping crown. Under harsher conditions it is only 5–7 m high with a sparse, open-canopied habit, and is usually associated with other plants such as Mulga, Native Orange, etc.

As is the case with many plants of the inland, the foliage is grey, the phyllodes being covered with a greyish white scurf. At the approach of rain, or when wet, the foliage emits a particularly offensive smell that can be almost unbearable. The phyllodes are lanceolate and up to 15 cm long with a curved mucro (point) and have many fine striate nerves. Bark is dark brown, rough, and deeply furrowed. The flower heads are not profuse, and are not a conspicuous feature of the tree. Seed pods are glabrous, and rather flat.

The timber is very hard and heavy, with a close, interlocked grain. It is noted for its durability and resistance to termites, and, among other things, is used extensively for fence posts. It is also an excellent firewood.

YARRAN *A. homalophylla* A. Cunn. ex Benth. is a close relative often confused with Gidgee. It has shorter phyllodes and different seed pods and seed arrangement, although Gidgee is mainly distinguished by the unpleasant smell of its foliage at certain times.

BRIGALOW *A. harpophylla* F. Muell. ex Benth. is another handsome tree wattle which is very common in inland Queensland and New South Wales where it forms large thickets known as 'Brigalow scrub'. It is a small to medium-sized tree with narrow, curved (falcate) greyish phyllodes and short racemes of globular yellow flower heads, normally appearing in late spring.

A. homalophylla

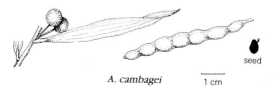

A. cambagei   1 cm

BLACK WATTLE

Acacia decurrens (J. Wendl.) Willd.
MIMOSACEAE

Black Wattle is a tree growing up to 14 m high usually found in the cool, moist hills and gullies of many parts of southern and eastern Australia.

This tree belongs to the large group of the *Acacia* genus known as *Bipinnatae*, i.e. those possessing feathery or bipinnate true leaves throughout their life. This group includes many trees and shrubs which, with a few exceptions, inhabit the wetter zones of the continent (over 500 mm rainfall).

Black Wattle is a graceful, handsome tree with rich green feathery foliage and smooth green smaller branches, but dark grey, almost black main trunk. Often spreading when given room, it is more commonly erect, and rather slender among other trees. The showy racemes of globular yellow flower heads arise from the leaf axils in great profusion in late winter, when the trees are a delight to behold. Seed pods, 5–10 cm long, are flattened, slightly curved, and constricted between the seeds.

This species, once extensively planted for tanbark in South Africa, is now out of control in that country, and known as the 'Green Cancer'.

GREEN WATTLE *A. mearnsii* De Wild. is a closely related species native to the same regions, but often occurring on poorer soil types. It is easily distinguished by its softer, pubescent foliage, shorter, broader leaflets, and pale flower heads which appear in summer. It is also grown extensively in South Africa and elsewhere for its very valuable tanbark.

SILVER WATTLE *A. dealbata* Link. is another commonly cultivated tree, rather similar, but with a mealy powder on the leaves and smaller branches, giving a silvery effect. The flower heads, which are a pale lemon, appear about the same time as those of *A. decurrens*.

All species mentioned are ornamental trees, particularly when young. They can be grown in drier conditions, but their life span and beauty are considerably increased in cool, moist situations akin to their natural environment.

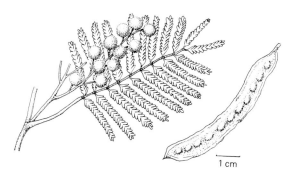

1 cm

IRONWOOD

Acacia estrophiolata F. Muell.
MIMOSACEAE

Ironwood is a dry area, inland tree, occurring in the north of South Australia west of Oodnadatta, and fairly commonly in central Australia.

The common name of Ironwood is applied to several other Australian trees, all of which possess a very hard timber. This tree is no exception, although the timber is perhaps no harder than that of Mulga and other inland acacias with which it is associated.

It is usually a long-lived tree, and a series of growth stages takes place before its final form is attained. During the first years of its life it is a rather prickly, unattractive shrub. As it develops it becomes a small, dense tree, finally becoming a mature weeping specimen about 10 m high. The long, pendulous, branching habit makes this tree a conspicuous and beautiful feature of certain parts of the central Australian landscape.

The foliage is a light grey-green, phyllodes being fairly long (5–8 cm), narrow, and glabrous. Flower heads are globular and small, and not a conspicuous feature of the tree. Seed pods are rather narrow and flat, the seeds disc-shaped.

Ironwood is usually found in heavy clay soils where it can be seen as a stately, single specimen tree, or in groups, or sometimes in colonies. These colonies are especially prevalent in the flats and depressions between ranges of hills where any runoff from the very infrequent rains is collected.

There are some particularly fine specimens of Ironwood in and around Alice Springs. To see these trees silhouetted against the fading light of day is a never-to-be-forgotten sight.

This tree would make a fine street or avenue tree for inland towns. In many respects it resembles the Drooping Myall (*A. pendula*).

Acacia excelsa Benth., also known as Ironwood, is a tree growing to 20 m, and one of the largest trees of the dry western plains of New South Wales and Queensland. This, too, is a particularly ornamental tree for dry conditions. In appearance it can be mistaken for the Mulga (*A. aneura* p.10).

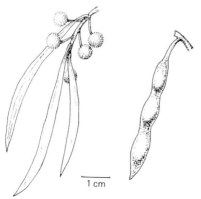

1 cm

SYDNEY GOLDEN WATTLE

Acacia longifolia Willd. var. *longifolia*
MIMOSACEAE

Sydney Golden Wattle is usually only a small tree. It is common in the coastal division of New South Wales, extending to the tablelands, but is also native to southern Queensland, Victoria, and Tasmania. It is also found in the wetter parts of South Australia, such as the Mount Lofty Ranges, but has naturalised itself in these parts from original plantings.

This is a variable plant, sometimes seen as a slender tree in shaded woodland or as a large bushy shrub; when single specimens are given room to expand, it sometimes sprawls to a remarkable spread of 10 m or more, with branches along the ground.

It can be a very handsome ornamental small tree up to 10 m in height with a dense, bushy crown, and bright green, shiny foliage, paler at the young tips. Phyllodes are long (7–15 cm), rather broadly lanceolate or obovate, and striped with prominent longitudinal veins. The bark on the trunk and main branches is smoothish and dull grey. The lemon-coloured flowers occur in large, fluffy, cylindrical spikes up to 5 cm long, prolific in August. Seed pods are curled and twisted.

When seen at its best this is a particularly ornamental species. It prefers moist, acid soils, and although easily grown in other conditions seldom then produces the healthy green foliage that contrasts so well with the flowers.

COAST WATTLE *A. longifolia* Willd. var. *sophorae* F. Muell. is a coastal species which inhabits the coastal sand dunes of most of temperate Australia. Although only a sprawling, shrubby plant, it is particularly useful as a sand binder and should be cultivated in seaside gardens. The phyllodes are rather thick and fleshy, but otherwise it is much the same as *A. longifolia*.

GOSSAMER WATTLE, WHITE SALLOW WATTLE *A. floribunda* (Vent.) Willd. is another ornamental tree growing to 14 m which is closely related. It inhabits streams and moist gullies in New South Wales and Queensland coastal areas, often on rich alluvial soils. It is usually a shapelier tree than *A. longifolia* with narrower drooping foliage and masses of pale yellow or cream flower spikes in early spring.

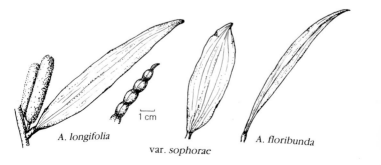

A. longifolia

var. *sophorae*

1 cm

A. floribunda

BLACKWOOD

Acacia melanoxylon R. Br.
MIMOSACEAE

Blackwood is a forest tree mainly found in the cool, moist, temperate regions of south-eastern Australia, but also extending to a subtropical climate in northern New South Wales and southern Queensland. It is found in the Mount Lofty Ranges and the wetter parts of the south-east in South Australia, over practically the whole of Tasmania, and in Victoria, New South Wales, and Queensland. Usually it is found as an understorey species in the large eucalypt forests where rainfall is 750–1800 mm annually.

It can be a fine, erect tree 25–30 m high, but is more often 16 m or less, with a trunk 30–100 cm in diameter. The branches begin well down the main trunk, are horizontal or slightly pendulous, and culminate in a dense rounded crown, the overall effect being very handsome. Bark is dark grey, rough, and furrowed, persistent to the smaller branches. Phyllodes are long and curved, bluntly pointed but tapering to the base, dark to pale green and leathery, with rather prominent longitudinal veins. The cream flower balls are in short axillary racemes, and appear in September. Seed pods are brown, flattened, and contorted, the black seeds within encircled by a bright red doubly folded funicle.

Blackwood timber is a prized fancy hardwood and is much sought after as a veneer for furniture and for other decorative purposes. It is usually a dark brown colour, and frequently beautifully figured. The main source of Blackwood timber is Tasmania, but even there it is now in limited supply.

The tree favours deep, moist soils in a cool to mild climate. Under such conditions it forms a handsome, shapely specimen tree well worth cultivating as an ornamental evergreen.

HICKORY *A. implexa* Benth. is a very similar tree that grows in similar locations. Its leaves are more pointed, the branches more rounded, and the seed funicles pale-coloured and folded under the seed where they are attached to the pod; otherwise it is very difficult to distinguish from the Blackwood tree.

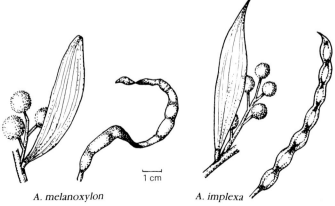

A. melanoxylon   *A. implexa*

WESTERN MYALL

Acacia papyrocarpa Benth.
(syn. *A. sowdenii* Maiden)
MIMOSACEAE

Western Myall is a small tree of the low-rainfall areas, extending from an eastern limit of the Flinders Ranges in South Australia to Balladonia in Western Australia. In certain parts, such as the countryside near Whyalla and Port Augusta in South Australia, it is the dominant tree, and lends its own tough character to the countryside. Rainfall is 150–300 mm annually, and soils are usually very alkaline, or limy.

The tree is only 5–8 m high, with a dense, rounded crown, often broader than it is high. Sheep are fond of the foliage, and often nibble it off as high as they can reach, giving the tree a neatly trimmed, umbrella-like appearance.

Phyllodes are long and narrow with a curved point; they are a silvery grey in colour, and the young tips are silky. This silvery foliage ripples and shines in the sun and wind, and is very lovely. The bark is dark, almost black, and very rough. Flowering is spasmodic, but in a good year the trees come alive with masses of small deep yellow flower balls.

The dark brown timber is dense and hard, and sometimes used to make ornamental woodwork boxes for cigars and jewels.

Western Myall is a distinctive, long-lived tree, particularly suited to harsh conditions where few trees are able to survive. This tree has no recovery from fire and can be completely wiped out in areas of bushfire.

A. loderi Maiden, found near Broken Hill, is very similar.

DROOPING MYALL *A. pendula* A. Cunn. is another lovely long-lived tree from the dry western plains of New South Wales, inland Queensland, and north-west Victoria. It is larger than Western Myall, up to 14 m high, with rough bark, broader, knife-shaped (cultrate) phyllodes, and small yellow flower balls.

It has beautiful drooping foliage. The thin, well-clothed, smaller branches hang vertically downwards, producing a lovely effect.

Drooping Myall prefers alluvial or heavy clay soils, its presence being considered a sign of good land. It is an excellent fodder tree, and is also a favourite meal of the bagmoth caterpillar which has seriously affected large areas of Drooping Myall country.

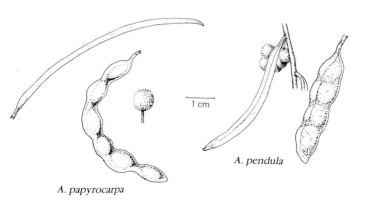

A. papyrocarpa

A. pendula

GOSFORD WATTLE, GOLDEN RAIN WATTLE

Acacia prominens A. Cunn.
MIMOSACEAE

Gosford Wattle is a lovely small to medium-sized tree native only to the east coast of New South Wales in the Sydney to Gosford districts.

Because of its ornamental appearance, however, it has found its way into cultivation, and is a reasonably well known species in other places where climate is suitable.

The tree is quite variable as regards size, sometimes only reaching about 5 m in height, but forming a fine, erect, well-branched tree of up to 25 m on the more fertile soils of adequate rainfall. It has an upright but short smooth grey trunk, and is well clothed with light grey-green rather silvery foliage, which is decorative at all times. The small slender racemes of inflorescences occur in early spring when the whole tree is covered in billowing masses of pale gold.

Phyllodes are 2·5–5 cm long, rather narrow, and slightly curved. Seed pods are straight, very flat, up to 10 cm long and a bluish colour.

This species does well as far south as Adelaide but prefers non-alkaline soils of assured rainfall. Under such conditions it should be more commonly cultivated than it is.

FRINGED WATTLE *A. fimbriata* A. Cunn. is a closely related species that is often found along river banks and in shady gullies in New South Wales and southern Queensland. It is just as attractive as Gosford Wattle, but seldom grows any larger than 5–7 m high. The foliage is a darker green, narrow and dainty, with a slightly drooping, lacy effect. The pale lemon flower balls are prolific and very beautiful. This species is adaptable and grows well in most soils receiving moderate rainfall.

BOX-LEAF WATTLE *A. buxifolia* A. Cunn. is another beautiful related species with glaucous box-like phyllodes and deep yellow flower heads, but it is usually only a shrub, seldom exceeding 3 m in height. It is found in Queensland, New South Wales, and Victoria.

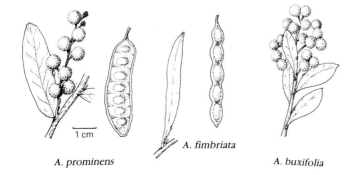

A. prominens

1 cm

A. fimbriata

A. buxifolia

GOLDEN WATTLE

Acacia pycnantha Benth.
MIMOSACEAE

Of all the species of *Acacia* that enliven the Australian bushland and roadsides after a drab winter, Golden Wattle perhaps rightly deserves top billing, at least in southern temperate Australia. This species is Australia's floral emblem.

The tree is not found in Western Australia, but is very prevalent throughout the temperate regions of South Australia and Victoria where rainfall is at least 350 mm and up to 1000 mm annually. It is also native to the extreme south-west of New South Wales, but has naturalised itself in the lower tablelands of that State. It regenerates very freely, particularly after fire, and frequently occurs in dense thickets of spindly plants as an understorey to eucalypt forest, or as a soil binder on denuded roadside cuttings. It is often seen at its best on very poor soils.

Golden Wattle is only a small tree, or sometimes a shrub, seldom exceeding about 8 m in height. The trunk is short and thin, the crown spreading, with rather upright branches. Bark is dark brown and rather smooth. It is extremely valuable for its tanning properties and has been extensively cultivated for this purpose, particularly overseas.

The phyllodes appear at a very early age, when they are particularly broad and large. Later they revert to a sickle or curved shape (falcate), rather broad, but variable. They are leathery and shining, a bright green in colour.

The large racemes of deep yellow, fluffy flower balls are highly perfumed, and occur on thick stalks. They are prominently displayed and very striking when massed above the glossy green foliage. Seed pods are 7–12 cm long by 6 mm broad, dark brown, and slightly constricted between the seeds.

Although often a magnificent bush specimen, Golden Wattle does not take kindly to cultivation, where it is frequently the subject of gall attack and does not flower well. It grows very rapidly with usually only a short life when cultivated.

A. gillii Maiden & Blakely is a South Australian species from Eyre Peninsula with very narrow phyllodes, but otherwise very similar to *A. pycnantha*.

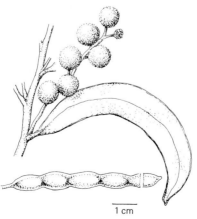

1 cm

NATIVE WILLOW, COOBA, BROUGHTON WILLOW

Acacia salicina Lindl.
MIMOSACEAE

Native Willow has an extensive range in the dry inland regions of all mainland States where it is found, from tropical Western Australia to north-west Victoria. The tree favours watercourses or clay depressions, but is found on most soils of the low rainfall areas. It seldom exceeds 14 m, but in places grows to a large tree 28 m tall.

As its common name implies, it is a tree with a drooping, willowy habit which is very beautiful. One wonders why this tree is not used more as a substitute for the very vigorous-rooted Weeping Willow (*Salix*). Although not deciduous, it is just as beautiful, and less troublesome. The tree is relatively slow growing and not so attractive in its early stages, features which probably restrict its popularity.

Native Willow has a shapely, rounded crown, with branches which droop to near ground level, providing ample shade. The bark is brown or grey, smooth and fissured. Phyllodes are long and narrow (up to 20 cm) and rather fleshy. The cream inflorescences in spring are not a conspicuous feature of the tree.

The tree suckers freely from the roots and is a useful soil binder in arid parts, although this feature can be a nuisance in cultivation.

It is a lovely, ornamental, and relatively long-lived species, which will grow in most soils, and can withstand long periods without rain. Along with the myalls (*A. pendula* and *A. papyrocarpa*) it possesses a rare Australian beauty that is seldom appreciated, at least for garden planting. When fully grown it makes a fine specimen tree.

UMBRELLA BUSH, SMALL COOBA *A. ligulata* A. Cunn. ex Benth. is a closely related, shrubby species, once regarded as a variety of *A. salicina*. It is widespread, usually occurring in dry, alkaline soils or coastal sand dunes. It flowers in profusion, with masses of orange-yellow flower balls, produced in August–September.

RIVER COOBA, EUMONG *A. stenophylla* A. Cunn. ex Benth. is somewhat similar to Native Willow but is usually more slender in growth. It inhabits inland watercourses, often in association with River Red Gum. This tree has very long, narrow drooping phyllodes, up to 35 cm long, and is a particularly ornamental tree when seen at its best.

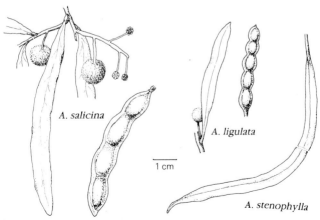

A. salicina

A. ligulata

1 cm

A. stenophylla

GOLDEN WREATH WATTLE, WILLOW WATTLE

Acacia saligna (Labill.) H. Wendl.

MIMOSACEAE

Golden Wreath Wattle is an extensively cultivated small, bushy tree noted for its rapidity of growth. Under favourable conditions it can reach tree size, 5–8 m high, in 4–5 years after planting out as a small seedling.

The tree is native to Western Australia, where it is often encountered along roadsides and elsewhere, in areas of at least moderate rainfall (400–800 mm annually). It has quite an extensive habitat range in the south-west, being found throughout the wheatlands and also in the Darling Range and Jarrah country, often where its roots are close to water.

There is a certain amount of confusion over the naming of this tree, some authorities listing it as the same species as Orange Wattle (*A. cyanophylla* Lindl.), another Western Australian small tree or large shrub, which has no apparent differences. Whether it is a separate species or not, there are two distinct forms of Golden Wreath Wattle in cultivation, one upright and slender, with an umbrella-like crown; the other dense and low-growing, usually with a thick, leaning trunk and rather heavy pendulous branches drooping to near the ground. Bark is rough, furrowed, and dark brown, but smooth and green on the small branchlets. Phyllodes are long, narrow, and ribbony with a prominent midrib, and are dull dark green or blue-green in colour.

During October the tree is loaded down with axillary racemes of very large, globular yellow flower heads, which make a spectacular show. The seeds germinate very freely and young plants can often be found under mature trees in their hundreds.

Golden Wreath Wattle is a particularly hardy tree, growing equally well on most soil types and in areas where rainfall varies from as low as 250 mm up to 1000 mm annually. It is an excellent tree as a quick shelter or to screen an ugly view in the garden, but cannot be considered permanent, as its life span is usually only 12–20 years. Sometimes the life is prolonged in dry situations where growth is slower.

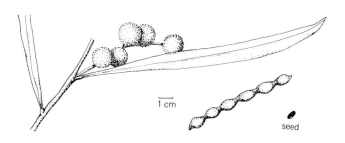

seed

1 cm

BAOBAB, BOAB, BOTTLE TREE

Adansonia gregorii F. Muell.
BOMBACACEAE

Among the world's most unusual trees, the Baobabs are often described as grotesque because of their huge, swollen, bottle-shaped trunks supporting a shallow crown of ungainly branches.

There are about twelve species, of which only one, *A. gregorii*, occurs in Australia. Other species are found in the hot, dry, savanna country of Africa and Malagasy, the gigantic Baobab of Africa (*A. digitata*) being the best-known. The Australian Baobab is similar but smaller. It occurs only in the monsoonal north-west of the continent, where these bare-limbed trees are a distinctive feature of the Kimberley landscape. The range extends to the Victoria River district in the Northern Territory.

At its best this tree reaches 14 m in height with sometimes a trunk girth up to 20 m. The trunk is often hollow, the spongy wood acting as a storage reservoir for water. The Prison Tree near Derby is a famous Baobab with an enormous hollowed trunk reputed to have been used as an overnight cell for prisoners.

The Baobab is deciduous, losing its leaves at the beginning of the 'dry' winter season when its large, hairy, gourd-like fruits are displayed conspicuously against the usually blue sky. Each fruit contains many kidney-shaped dark brown or black seeds embedded in a pleasant-tasting white pulp which is eaten by Aboriginals and has given rise to several common names including 'Cream-of-Tartar Tree.' In Africa, it is also called 'Monkey Bread' because of the native monkeys' liking for the fruit. When diluted with hot water, the pulp makes a pleasant drink, and it has been fermented by bushmen to produce an alcoholic beverage akin to the famous 'jungle juice' (from coconuts) of World War II.

Cattle will eat most parts of the fallen tree, including the fibrous wood.

Because of the unpleasant steamy weather of the 'wet' monsoonal season, this tree is not often seen in leaf by travellers, who are inclined to avoid the area at that time of the year. However, its large palmate leaves of 5–9 pointed leaflets and its beautiful creamy white, sweetly scented solitary flowers are attractive features which are only produced during the 'wet', and then not every year. The flowers have silky calyces and five fleshy petals surrounding many long white stamens.

Baobabs live to a very great age, a feature which is evident when the very old trees are compared with their young, slender and less grotesque counterparts.

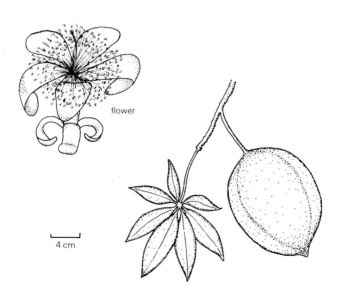

flower

4 cm

QUEENSLAND KAURI PINE

Agathis robusta (C. Moore ex F. Muell.) Bailey
ARAUCARIACEAE

Queensland Kauri Pine is one of Australia's most important timber trees and continues to be extensively logged from the dwindling native rainforests. It is one of only three recorded Australian *Agathis* species, all endemic. The genus is also, however, represented in the south-west Pacific, Malaysia, and New Zealand, where the Kauri pines are legendary.

The genus is distinguished from *Araucaria* (pp.56–59) by the stalked flat leaves with a blunt apex (these are quite different from those of *Araucaria*, which are more crowded and spirally arranged) and the winged seeds, which are free from the cone scale (in *Araucaria* they are united and enclosed within the cone scale).

Queensland Kauri Pine is a large, tall and erect, symmetrical tree with a long straight trunk clothed with smooth to flaky grey-brown bark. Branches are ascending and the leaves smooth and flat, 10–15 cm long by 2–3 cm wide, normally narrowly ovate to lanceolate, with parallel veins and a rounded apex. The male and female 'flowering' cones are frequently borne on the same tree about August. The female fruiting cones which follow are very large, up to 15 cm long by 8–10 cm across, and ovoid to cylindrical in shape. Seeds are flat and winged, maturing in summer.

Kauri is an attractive softwood timber suited to many indoor uses, including fancy cabinet work.

Confined to limited areas of southern Queensland, including Fraser Island, with a northern extremity in the Atherton district, this tree is no longer very plentiful.

In cultivation it forms a tall, stately tree which has been used spasmodically in parks and large gardens and has succeeded in areas as far south as Adelaide and Melbourne. Young trees are susceptible to frost, and seedlings tend to grow slowly for the first 2 years or so.

The other two recorded species, *A. microstachya* Bailey & C. T. White and *A. atropurpurea* Hyland, are similar large, erect forest trees found only in north Queensland, mainly on the Atherton Tableland. They have smaller leaves and cones than *A. robusta*, the cones being particularly small (about 5 cm long) in *A. atropurpurea*.

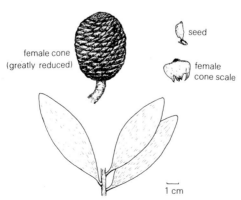

female cone
(greatly reduced)

seed

female
cone scale

1 cm

WESTERN AUSTRALIAN WILLOW MYRTLE

Agonis flexuosa (Sprengel) Schauer
MYRTACEAE

The Western Australian Willow Myrtle is a small tree prevalent throughout the wetter Jarrah and Karri forest country of south-western Western Australia, including the Swan Coastal Plain where Perth is situated. The tree usually inhabits moist sandy soils, and is sometimes found in swamps.

It seldom exceeds 10–15 m in height. When young it is a slender, drooping, single-stemmed tree that eventually produces a more spreading umbrageous crown of drooping willow-like habit. The trunk and branches are grey or dark brown with rough, furrowed bark. The tree lives to a great age, when the trunk often becomes very thick and gnarled, with only a few upper branches. The leaves are quite broad and shining in the early stages with bronzy red new growth, but eventually revert to dark green; they are narrow and willowy with a pleasantly aromatic myrtle scent.

Flowers are small and white, but numerous, and clothe the hanging branches so that they appear to be covered with tiny white stars during spring months.

This tree is widely cultivated as a specimen tree, often used in place of the introduced Weeping Willow (*Salix*), which has such a voracious root system as to render it undesirable in small suburban gardens. It is very adaptable and will grow on most soils including sands and silts in seaside areas.

All the *Agonis* species found in Australia are native to the south-west of Western Australia, and most are only of shrub size.

Agonis juniperina Schauer is one that can reach small tree proportions, usually only about 7 m. It is a slender, rough-barked tree of juniper-like foliage with very tiny leaves and small white star flowers in spring, but it is unlike the Western Australian Willow Myrtle in general appearance. It is quite ornamental and easy to cultivate.

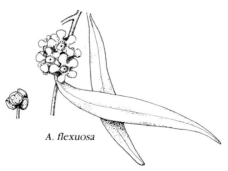

A. flexuosa

1 cm

A. juniperina

SAFE SIRIS, WOMEN'S TONGUES

Albizia procera Benth.

MIMOSACEAE

This attractive, graceful tree is a common species on the hill-sides around Cairns and in eucalypt forests along the Cook Highway north of Cairns.

Most albizias are free-flowering, attractive trees, about ten species being listed as native to Australia, although there is some uncertainty whether they are all indigenous, or escapes from outside Australia. The Australian species are mainly found in the warm areas of north Queensland. Safe Siris is native to India and most of tropical Asia as well as northern Australia, growing near the coast or on the fringes of rainforest. It is listed as occurring in Western Australia and the Northern Territory as well as Queensland.

In Australia, this tree is rarely seen taller than 10–12 m high, with an open crown of ornamental pinnate foliage. An added attraction is its near-white bark. It is semideciduous; extra watering in the 'dry' season (winter) delays leaf fall. The leaves are bipinnate, having 2–3 pairs of leaflets, with 6–9 pairs of pinnules in each leaflet. The pinnules are 2–4 cm long, oblong, blunt-ended and narrowed at the base, on a short stalk.

Flowering is prolific, the flowers appearing from October to January in loose terminal panicles; each panicle is globular and greenish or creamy white in colour. The flowers are delicately perfumed.

The flowers are followed by numerous flat fruiting pods, 10–20 cm long by about 2 cm wide, and reddish pink in colour. These hang on the tree for a long period in winter and clack together in the wind, giving rise to the sometimes used common name of Women's Tongues.

Safe Siris is sometimes grown in Darwin, but is not well known in cultivation. It is adaptable to soil types, rapid growing and easily propagated by seed or cuttings. It is frost-tender and should be avoided in areas of frost risk, but it is well suited to planting in warm tropical areas near the coast. It appears to retain its attractive tree form under most conditions, but because of its soft wood, it is prone to attacks from borers and termites, a fault of most of the albizias.

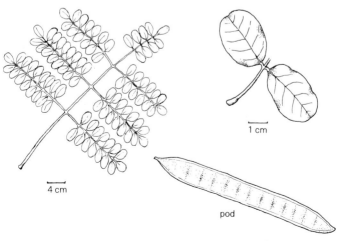

4 cm

1 cm

pod

DESERT OAK

Allocasuarina decaisneana (F. Muell.) L. Johnson
CASUARINACEAE

Desert Oak is one of the loveliest of all the she-oak or casuarina trees. It is an inhabitant of the dry inland areas of central Australia where it is almost always found growing in the red sand dunes.

In 1982 the family Casuarinaceae was revised by Dr L. Johnson of the National Herbarium of New South Wales, resulting in a family of four genera. The changes included the separation of the genus *Casuarina* into two: *Allocasuarina* and *Casuarina*.

The botanical differences are of a minor nature and perhaps the most readily distinguishable of these is in the body of the samara (fruit) which carries the seeds. It is brown or black in *Allocasuarina*, and grey or silvery in *Casuarina*.

The general characteristics of *Allocasuarina* are the same as those of *Casuarina* and these are described under *Casuarina cunninghamiana* (p.108).

Desert Oak varies in each stage of its growth. In its juvenile form it is fastigiate in habit, and rather tall and slender. As it matures it begins to develop a denser habit, but it is not until it reaches full maturity that its characteristic shape is finally acquired.

Usually a tree up to 10 m in height, it occasionally grows higher. Its spread varies considerably, but the tree can be as broad as it is high. It has a graceful weeping habit, characteristic of the she-oak group.

The foliage is usually a dull green that blends perfectly with the background colour of the red sand dunes with which it is usually associated. Its straight trunk is dark brown, almost black, and very deeply furrowed.

The seed cones which are produced on the female trees are the largest in the genus, about 5 cm or more long and up to 4 cm in width. Timber is very strong and durable.

Little is known about Desert Oak as a cultivated tree, but its reluctance to grow anywhere but on deep sand would indicate that perfect drainage is required for its successful growth.

The sight of the Desert Oak on red sand dunes near Mount Olga and Ayers Rock, or backed by the blue Mann Ranges, is surely enough to inspire appreciation of one of the most striking trees of dry inland Australia.

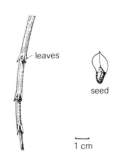

leaves

seed

1 cm

BLACK SHE-OAK

Allocasuarina littoralis (Salisb.) L. Johnson
CASUARINACEAE

In flower, the male form of this tree is one of the loveliest to be found among the casuarina family. The photograph depicts this feature very clearly as a male tree is shown in full bloom in May, when it lights up forest bushland with its colourful deep orange-bronze to rusty red flowers enveloping the whole tree.

The tree is an inhabitant of mainly moist eucalypt forests of the east coast regions, extending from Tasmania to Cape York Peninsula in Queensland. It is a common understorey tree along road verges of the Pacific Highway. At certain times the tree takes on a dark or blackish appearance, from which the common name is derived.

It normally grows to a fairly slender but erect tree, 3–8 m high, occasionally larger, with finely fissured dark grey bark and the typical lacy foliage of the she-oaks. The leaves are the small teeth arranged around the joints of the soft, segmented branchlets (cladodes).

Male and female flowers occur on separate trees. The female inflorescences are small, red and cone-shaped, and are not showy. The male flowers, by contrast, are borne in terminal spikes which literally cover the whole tree, as described above, over a long period during late autumn and winter.

The woody seed cones are produced on the female trees only. These are 2–2·5 cm long, are of roughly cylindrical shape and contain the typical winged seeds of she-oaks.

Timber is red, hard and durable, and has an ornamental grain suitable for fancy veneers and interior furniture.

This genus is propagated from seed, and it is not possible to determine whether the seedling is male or female until it is large enough to flower. This is a pity, as it is the male trees that would gain most attention in cultivation. Nonetheless, the Black She-oak is an attractive-foliaged tree well suited to ornamental planting in areas of assured rainfall and good drainage.

seed

1 cm

FOREST OAK, ROSE SHE-OAK

Allocasuarina torulosa (Ait.) L. Johnson
CASUARINACEAE

Forest Oak is a slender, pyramidal tree of the coastal eucalyptus forests of eastern Australia extending from Cairns in northern Queensland to as far south as Nowra in New South Wales.

Most of this habitat is subtropical in climate with mainly summer rainfall, although in its southern extremity, and on the tablelands in New South Wales, frosts are not uncommon, and there is some snow at the higher altitudes.

Although found at sea-level, Forest Oak is more commonly encountered in hilly country, usually on moist fertile soils, and mainly as a secondary species to forest eucalypts such as Sydney Blue Gum (*E. saligna*). Annual rainfall is 750–1250 mm.

Depending on conditions the tree varies from 10 to 25 m in height with an erect, slender, rough trunk, and wispy, drooping, rather open foliage. The dark grey bark is rough and persistent on both trunk and main branches, closely furrowed down and across, and corky. The fine, wispy, needle-like cladodes are sometimes pinkish when young, a very attractive feature of the tree from which it gets its common name, Rose She-oak. The woody cones enclosing the fruits are globular or barrel-shaped, about 1·5–2·5 cm in diameter.

The timber is hard and durable, and can be given an ornamental appearance when used for veneers and joinery. Like the wood of most casuarinas, it burns with great heat and was once prized as fuel.

Because of its habit and coloured foliage this is an extremely ornamental tree suited for planting in areas of assured rainfall. It does well as far south as South Australia, particularly in the cooler areas such as the Mount Lofty Ranges where it seldom grows any larger than a slender 8–12 m tree.

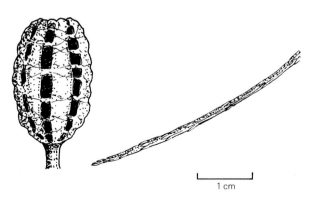

1 cm

DROOPING SHE-OAK

Allocasuarina verticillata (Lam.) L. Johnson
CASUARINACEAE

Drooping She-oak is a relatively small-growing tree inhabiting many parts of southern and eastern temperate Australia. It is found in New South Wales, Victoria, South Australia, and Tasmania.

This tree is often seen along the coast in calcareous sands which are subjected to a fierce buffeting by salt-laden winds. Further inland it occurs on poor rocky soils where it is often the dominant tree in areas with about 350 mm rainfall, but it is seen at its best in open forest country of moderate rainfall. Here soils are usually sand, often overlying a clay subsoil.

The tree has a single erect trunk, with rough, persistent dark grey bark and a compact, bushy crown of pendulous foliage which gives dense shade. The long, ribbed, needle-like branches are dark green and droop significantly, giving the tree its attractive and characteristic weeping appearance. Usually only 5–8 m high, it sometimes reaches 14 m.

Male specimens often flower profusely in late autumn, when they are smothered in small golden brown or rust-coloured flowers. The effect is one of the loveliest produced by any Australian tree. When the flowers drop and cover the ground beneath the tree the effect is still almost as lovely. Fruiting cones are dark grey, rather large (up to 5 cm long), and oval-shaped with prominent valves.

Adaptable to most soils and situations, Drooping She-oak is a fine farm, shade and shelter tree. It should also be cultivated more for ornament, particularly in difficult coastal sites and windy situations where the choice of trees is limited.

WESTERN AUSTRALIAN SHE-OAK *A. fraseriana* (Miq.) L. Johnson is a very handsome species native to moist sandy soils in the south-west. It forms a lovely small tree with deep, lustrous green foliage and a smoother trunk than most trees of the genus.

BULL OAK or **BULOKE** *A. luehmannii* (R. T. Baker) L. Johnson is a common tall erect tree found in moderately dry inland areas of eastern Australia.

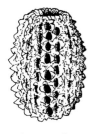

leaves

seed

male flowers

A. verticillata

1 cm

A. fraseriana

A. luehmanni

MILKY PINE, WHITE CHEESEWOOD

Alstonia scholaris (L.) R. Br.

APOCYNACEAE

Apart from its often conical or pyramidal shape, Milky Pine bears no other resemblance to the pines or other conifer species. In fact, younger trees are characteristically seen displaying a habit very similar to that of the Native Frangipani (*Hymenosporum*, p. 234), with an upright trunk or several main trunks together and tiers of horizontal radiating branches, each well-clothed with leaves in whorls. The writer sometimes mistook it for that species when travelling by car. On closer examination, however, it is quite different, the smooth leaves being much thicker and fig-like in appearance. The leaves have whorls of four to eight leaflets, each narrowly elliptical; the latter are dark shiny green with a paler reverse, a prominent midrib and evenly spaced parallel veins at right angles to the midrib. Leaflets are usually 12–20 cm long by 3–5 cm wide, and are shorter near the base of the leaf.

Milky Pine is a common tree of lowland rainforest, extending from south of Mackay to Thursday Island. It also occurs outside Australia, extending as far as India. It is very commonly encountered because it is one of the few rainforest trees often left as solitary specimens on farms and plantations, when its appearance is always attractive.

At its best the tree reaches 30 m with an upright trunk which is flanged at the base, but most trees seen are much smaller than this, often having foliage near the ground. The bark is light grey and when cut exudes quantities of milky sap, as do the branchlets and leaves when broken, hence its common name.

Unfortunately the writer was unable to obtain flowers or fruits to sketch but the flowers are described as cream, fragrant and tubular with bell-shaped calyces, over 1 cm long and occurring in large clusters at the ends of the branches from October to December. The fruit is a long, thin, papery, two-lobed follicle up to 30 cm long. Hanging down like beans or straps, the fruits are a distinguishing feature of the tree. The papery seeds have tufts of long hairs at each end.

The timber of the Milky Pine is creamy white, very soft and porous, but is used in cabinet work and for other timber products.

This is a fast-growing, ornamental tree for deep, moist soils, although it will tolerate drier conditions, where trees are smaller and slower in growth.

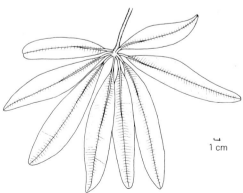

1 cm

SMOOTH-BARKED APPLE, SYDNEY APPLE, RED GUM

Angophora costata (Gaertn.) Britten
MYRTACEAE

This is one of the best-loved trees of the Sydney area, where it is common on the Hawkesbury Sandstone that is prevalent in parts of that city. Here it is often seen with a thick, smooth but dimpled, orange- or pink-barked trunk and massive twisted roots exposed above the rocks in which it grows. The crown is spreading, often with many irregularly curving, thick limbs, particularly on the older trees, which develop informal artistic shapes of rugged attractiveness.

This tree is, however, by no means confined to the Sydney area, extending along the coastal regions of northern New South Wales and occurring more commonly in Queensland, where it enjoys an extensive range along the coast. Smooth-barked Apple sheds its mature greyish bark annually to expose the richly coloured new bark described above. It grows from about 15 to 25 m high with a trunk at the base sometimes in excess of 1 m in diameter. The opposite leaves are sessile and very furry at first, but the adult leaves are smooth on short stalks, lanceolate or narrowly oblong; the new growing tips are a bright red. Venation is parallel.

The creamy white flowers of this species can be very showy, held prominently above the foliage in terminal corymbs; they usually appear in early summer and are of short duration. Buds and stalks are covered with short bristles. The ovoid fruit is a capsule, 1 cm or more in length, eucalypt-like but not as woody, with prominent ribs. It contains fairly large, broad, flat seeds.

Timber is brownish and straight-grained, but it is not very durable and is not used much, except for firewood.

Smooth-barked Apple is a very ornamental tree which is easily cultivated in most soils. It grows readily well outside its natural habitat range in areas such as Adelaide and Melbourne, where some fine specimens can be found.

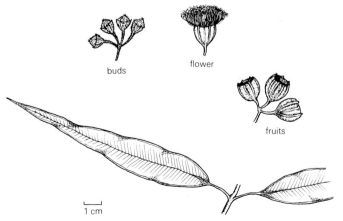

buds

flower

fruits

1 cm

ROUGH-BARKED APPLE

Angophora floribunda (Smith) Sweet
(syn. *A. intermedia* DC.)
MYRTACEAE

Often mistaken for eucalyptus trees, particularly the blood-wood group, which they closely resemble in general appearance, angophoras are principally inhabitants of the wetter parts of New South Wales and Queensland.

Rough-barked Apple is widespread along the east coast from southern Queensland to north-west Victoria. In New South Wales it is also found scattered throughout the mountainous areas below 1200 m, and extends to the beginning of the dry western plains. The best climate for it is subtropical to temperate, with rainfall 500–1000 mm and alluvial or deep sandy loam soils.

It is a rather short-trunked, wide-spreading tree 14–24 m high, with gnarled branches in older specimens. Bark is brown, persistent to the smaller branches, thick and fibrous.

The genus is mainly distinguished from *Eucalyptus* by the undeveloped flowers, which have no operculum, or cap. The fruits, moreover, are ribbed, thin, and rather papery or fragile. Trees are free-flowering with showy panicles of cream flowers prominently displayed in summer.

Eucalyptus leaves are usually, but not always, alternate and scattered, whereas those of all species of *Angophora* are in opposite pairs. The leaves of this fine tree are bright green and show up conspicuously among other associated trees in forest stands.

Rough-barked Apple is an adaptable tree, useful for shade, shelter, and ornament.

BROAD-LEAVED APPLE *A. subvelutina* F. Muell. is another ornamental species. It is a very similar rough-barked tree, but is easily distinguished by its stalkless leaves which are heart-shaped at the base.

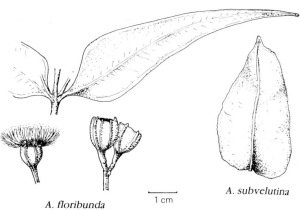

A. floribunda

1 cm

A. subvelutina

BUNYA PINE

Araucaria bidwillii Hook.
ARAUCARIACEAE

Bunya Pine belongs to the group of well-known subtropical softwood trees collectively known as kauri pines. This group consists of *Agathis robusta* (Queensland Kauri Pine), *Araucaria cunninghamii* (Hoop Pine), and the Bunya Pine. These are all fine timber trees native to the rainforests of eastern Australia, mainly Queensland, the Hoop Pine extending to New Guinea. They are often a feature of the skyline, towering over other species in the rainforests where they occur.

Bunya Pine has a very restricted natural distribution, and is only found in Queensland between Gympie and the Bunya Mountains, with an isolated occurrence much further north near Port Douglas. The tree favours rich volcanic soils, preferably in moist valleys and at low elevations. Rainfall is 370–1250 mm, mainly in summer. Bunya Pine always occurs as a scattered tree dominating other species in the area. It is a particularly striking tree, growing to 50 m with a large symmetrical dome-shaped crown like an elongated beehive.

The 60–120 cm diameter trunk is a long, straight, cylindrical bole, tapering only slightly to the top of the tree. The branches which radiate from the trunk are almost horizontal, but with a slight downward trend. They converge towards the top of the tree. The dark grey bark is hard and rough over the trunk and branches and is cracked into thin, horizontal scales. The crowded, hard, dark green leaves are flat and glossy, and spiral from the branchlets.

The male 'flowers', which are long thin spikes at the ends of the branchlets, appear in September–October on the same tree as the female 'flowers'. These arise laterally from the branchlets and are composed of crowded carpels which develop into fruiting cones. These cones are pineapple-shaped, large and woody, up to 30 cm long by about 20 cm in diameter. They contain large seeds with a milky flesh and were once relished by the Aboriginals.

Bunya Pine yields a similar timber to the other kauri pines, all of which are prominent Australian softwoods.

Although too large for average gardens, it is occasionally planted as a park tree and grows successfully as far south as Adelaide provided there is adequate moisture.

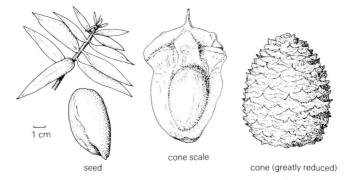

1 cm

seed

cone scale

cone (greatly reduced)

HOOP PINE

Araucaria cunninghamii Ait. ex D. Don
ARAUCARIACEAE

Only two species of *Araucaria* are found in mainland Australia, *A. bidwillii* (Bunya Pine, p. 56) and the Hoop Pine, although the Norfolk Island Pine (*A. excelsa*) is well known in cultivation, particularly at beach resorts. Hoop Pine is found naturally along the coast and adjacent mountains of northern New South Wales to northern Queensland.

The genus has other representatives in South America and the Pacific Islands.

The araucarias are distinctive among the conifers because of their erect, mast-like trunks supporting evenly distributed branches which become increasingly smaller towards the top of the tree. Hoop Pine is typical in this respect, the small, sharply pointed, crowded leaves forming rich green clusters of foliage on stiffly angled branches symmetrical about the upright trunk. It matures to a large majestic tree to 50 m high, but is slow-growing when young. Bark is brown and rough.

Both male and female 'flowers' occur on the same tree, usually in summer. The woody female cones which are formed after flowering are large and egg-shaped, resembling a small, green pineapple prior to ripening. At maturity they turn brown and disintegrate, releasing the seeds. They then fall from the tree, usually in summer, leaving a thick central axis on the tree. Unlike the heavy seeds of the Bunya Pine, Hoop Pine seeds are wind-borne, and if seed is required, the cones should be collected just prior to ripening.

The pale yellowish timber of this tree was the principal native softwood and was used extensively for general indoor work, although its availability is becoming increasingly restricted.

A glaucous form of *A. cunninghamii* inhabits the islands of the Whitsunday Passage and northwards, being found in stunted form growing virtually to the edge of the sea.

In cultivation, Hoop Pine can be used as a large formal specimen tree in parks and large gardens. It is also useful as a pot or tub specimen because of its slow growth when young and particularly when its roots are confined.

It can be grown successfully as far south as Adelaide and Melbourne but is better suited to the rich loams of the east coast of northern Australia.

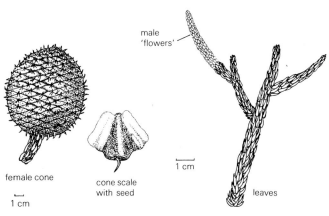

male 'flowers'

female cone

cone scale with seed

1 cm

1 cm

leaves

1 cm

BANGALOW PALM, PICCABEEN PALM

Archontophoenix cunninghamiana
(H. Wendl.) H. Wendl. & Drude
ARECACEAE

This is a tall palm which can still be admired in its natural set-
ting in places such as Mount Tamborine in southern Queensland. It is found naturally over an extensive range of the east
coast, from southern New South Wales to central Queensland,
where it is sometimes seen in small pure stands which have
been left uncleared. It favours wet situations such as gullies and
stream banks.

The trunk is smooth, tall and slender, up to 20 cm in
diameter, and slightly swollen at the base, usually bare for
about 20 m below the crown of feather-like fronds. The outer
fronds are graceful and pendulous, the central ones erect; the
individual linear-lanceolate leaflets are numerous and finely
divided, with a few large brown scales on the undersides.
Archontophoenix is characterised by these pinnate leaves with
leaflets evenly distributed in one plane, and with a sheath
completely encircling the trunk.

A feature of this palm is the inflorescences and the fruits
which follow. These surround the trunk below the leaves, in
dense branches with long pendulous branchlets. The very
numerous tightly sheathed flowers are pinkish yellow or purplish. The red or pink fruits are globular or ellipsoid, 10–15 mm
across, and resemble strings of beads hanging vertically around
the trunk in thick clusters.

Bangalows are noted for their ability to withstand cyclonic
winds. Their cabbages (apical buds) were relished by Aboriginals, who also used the expanded leaf base as a water carrier.
The tree was once called Pikki, after the Aboriginal name for
the leaf base; this was later expanded to Piccabeen.

ALEXANDRA PALM *A. alexandrae* H. Wendl. & Drude is a
somewhat similar palm from eastern Australia, extending as far
north as Cape York in Queensland. The trunk is usually prominently ringed, and more obviously swollen just above ground
level than that of the Bangalow Palm. The undersides of the
leaves are clothed with silvery scales, giving them a whitish
appearance (those of the Bangalow are green).

Both these palms are in cultivation and will succeed much further south than their natural range, provided water is assured.
They are also grown extensively as attractive container plants
for patios and greenhouses. They can be readily propagated
from seed.

leaflets evenly
distributed in
one plane

sheath completely
encircles trunk

leaf
(greatly
reduced)

leaflet

fruit shapes

TULIP OAK, BLACK JACK

Argyrodendron actinophyllum (Bailey) Edlin.
subsp. *actinophyllum*
STERCULIACEAE

One of the commonest trees of the mountainous rainforest scrubs of southern Queensland, particularly the Macpherson Range, Tulip Oak is also found as far south as Gloucester in New South Wales.

It is a tall, erect, stately tree up to 50 m in height with dense, glossy, handsome foliage. The trunk, usually about 1 m in diameter, has prominent, rather broad buttressing. Bark is dark brown, finely fissured, and shed in rather small flaky pieces. The very attractive compound leaves on long stalks are alternate, and consist of leaflets radiating from the top of the stalk in umbrella-like fashion. Although not as large or as thick and leathery, they are otherwise very similar to the leaves of the Umbrella Tree (*Schefflera actinophylla*, p. 294). The small white bell-shaped flowers have no petals and appear in long axillary panicles during April. Fruit is a carpel, 4–6 cm long, containing a rounded seed at the base with a thin flat wing near the top of the carpel.

There is only one other well-known species of *Argyrodendron* in Australia, although that particular species has a number of varieties mainly found in the tropical north of Queensland.

CROWSFOOT ELM *A. trifoliatum* F. Muell. is similar in size and habit to Tulip Oak. It is very common throughout the coastal scrubs, particularly of Queensland, but also of northern New South Wales. The thin-sectioned, web-like buttressing of this tree is a distinctive feature, and quite different from that of Tulip Oak. Crowsfoot Elm is easily recognised by its leaves, which consist of three leaflets 7–12 cm long, at the ends of long stalks. The undersides of the leaves, flowers, and branchlets are covered with small silvery or coppery scales.

Timber of both species is tough and straight-grained; it has many uses, but must be treated against borer attack.

Both trees can be successfully grown as far south as Adelaide in deep soils with assured water, but eventually they will grow too large for the average-sized garden.

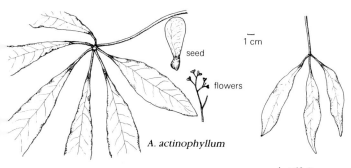

seed

flowers

1 cm

A. actinophyllum

A. trifoliatum

WHITEWOOD

Atalaya hemiglauca (F. Muell.) F. Muell. ex Benth.
SAPINDACEAE

This tree is widespread in the dry, inland parts of Australia, being found in all mainland States except Victoria. In these regions it is a useful shelter tree for stock and a source of stockfeed during drought, although its foliage has been found to be poisonous to horses. Poisoning is due to a water-soluble saponin. This is more prevalent in the northern parts of its range, but even here, the leaves have to be eaten in quantity to affect the horses unduly.

The common name of Whitewood is derived from the uniformly pale whitish or cream wood, which is soft and closely grained but appears to have no commercial use.

Only small, usually 5–9 m high, with often a good canopy of foliage, the tree is a rather handsome one when compared with many of its companions in its arid environment. Bark is smooth, or sometimes scaly and friable, pale grey or whitish in colour.

The leaves are variable: in their early stages they are simple or sometimes lobed, but at the adult stage they are pinnate with the narrow oblong-lanceolate leaflets in two to six opposite pairs, each leaflet 6–20 cm long. Their upper surface is a smooth, waxy green, but they are paler beneath, this feature giving rise to the specific epithet of *hemiglauca* (half grey).

In late winter to early spring the flowers are produced, occurring in large axillary or terminal panicles near the ends of the branchlets. Each flower is small, five-petalled, and reddish white in colour.

A distinctive feature of the tree is the two-winged dry fruits (samaras) which arise from the main hairy-segmented fruits when these split open. These are very similar to those of the well-known maples (*Acer*). The fruits are very toxic to horses, but fortunately are not palatable.

The genus *Atalaya* comprises only about four species, all Australian, although *A. salicifolia* extends to Timor where it is known as *atalay* and it is from this name that the botanical name *Atalaya* is derived.

To the author's knowledge, Whitewood is unknown in cultivation. It favours sandy or light loamy soils under natural conditions.

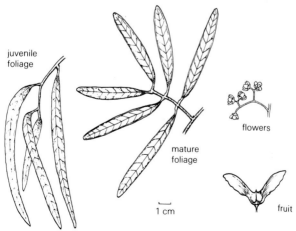

juvenile foliage

mature foliage

flowers

fruit

1 cm

KING WILLIAM PINE

Athrotaxis selaginoides D. Don
TAXODIACEAE

Native to the cool rainforests of south-west Tasmania, mature specimens of King William Pine are no longer common, owing to the demands for its very valuable softwood timber.

The genus is limited to two species only, these being the only representatives of the family Taxodiaceae in the Southern Hemisphere. This family includes the mighty sequoias or red-woods of North America, of which *Sequoia sempervirens* is the world's tallest tree.

King William Pine grows in a cool temperate climate with a rainfall of 1500–2500 mm annually, and with snow quite common in winter.

At its best it seldom reaches 35 m in height; it has a sparse crown of foliage, and often a forked trunk, sometimes but-tressed at the base. Bark is reddish brown and persistent, with a soft spongy texture, and longitudinally furrowed. The spirally arranged, small, crowded leaves are keeled and sharply pointed. Male and female 'flowers' occur on the same tree, terminal fruit-ing cones being stalkless, and reaching maturity in one season.

Timber is a very durable, easily worked softwood with a pleasant cedar scent. It has many uses.

The tree is very slow-growing and is unknown in cultivation.

The other species of the genus, *A. cupressoides* D. Don (Pencil Pine), is quite rare.

There are two other famous Tasmanian pines confined mainly to the south-western half, both slow-growing, excellent timber trees that are now in only limited supply.

HUON PINE *Dacrydium franklinii* Hook. f. is found mainly in swampy or moist soils of the river flats. It is usually a shaft-like tree under 35 m high, with a slightly rough, persistent grey bark, and thick, keeled, closely imbricate leaves. Fruiting cones are minute and near the ends of the branchlets. The timber contains a strongly scented resin that repels insects and makes it very valuable as well as light and tough.

CELERY TOP PINE *Phyllocladus asplenifolius* Hook. f. is usually a 20–35 m tree, sometimes dwarfed in exposed situ-ations, with foliage consisting of broadly wedge-shaped, lobed cladodes (flattened branchlets), the true leaves appearing as tiny scales along the edges of the cladodes.

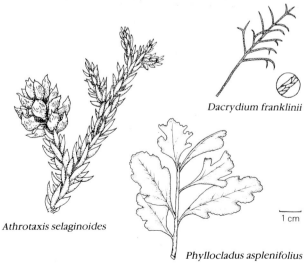

Dacrydium franklinii

Athrotaxis selaginoides

Phyllocladus aspleniifolius

1 cm

GREY MANGROVE

Avicennia marina (Forsk.) Vierh.
VERBENACEAE

Mangroves are an important feature of the vegetation in many parts of Australia. They grow along muddy seashores and tidal estuaries, and are usually found in dense stands known as mangrove swamps. These areas consist of salty, waterlogged mud which is frequently flooded by sea water and is intolerable to most plant life. These swamps act as a natural barrier, protecting other plants from the sea water and salt winds.

The area beneath the mangrove trees is often covered with a tangled jungle of long, arching roots which anchor the trees to the mud. As the root system develops, new growing shoots emerge and eventually form more trees, which in their turn repeat the process, thus producing a dense combination of enjoined trees. Under the trees peg-like, erect, aerial roots also project up through the mud; they absorb air at low tide. In this feature, *Avicennia* differs from *Rhizophora*, another genus of mangrove from tropical Australia, which sends aerial roots down from the branches to stay them to the muddy soil beneath.

Grey Mangrove is usually a stout, crooked, low-branching tree less than 7 m in height, and, in general shape, not unlike many banksia trees. Sometimes it grows to 14 m in height, but this is rare. The light grey bark is smooth and thin. The leaves are in opposite pairs, thick and broadly lanceolate, about 7·5 cm long, and bright glossy green with a white, silky undersurface. The tiny, orange, sessile flowers are on rigid stalks in axillary clusters, and are much loved by bees. They usually occur in summer. Mangrove honey has a distinctive and pleasing flavour. Fruits consist of a small two-valved capsule containing one seed which germinates before dropping, usually vertically, in the mud. The timber is used in boat building.

The several other species of mangrove in Australia belong to different genera, and are usually found in subtropical or tropical areas. *Avicennia officinalis* L., a closely related species, is now considered native to India, China, and the near East, but not to Australia.

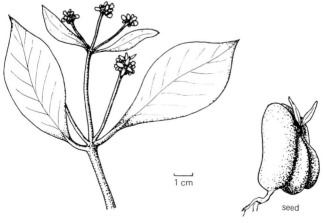

seed

GIANT BANKSIA

Banksia grandis Willd.
PROTEACEAE

Giant Banksia, so named because of its giant flower spikes and leaves, both often over 30 cm in length, is perhaps the most commonly encountered of all the western banksia trees. It extends from some 320 km north of Perth, through the lateritic gravelly soils of the Darling Range as an understorey tree in eucalypt forest, and through the Jarrah and Karri forests (sometimes with its base totally immersed in water during winter) to the south coast near Albany. Here it appears with Jarrah in a stunted form on rocky granite slopes or limestone cliffs.

The genus *Banksia* commemorates the name of Sir Joseph Banks and is entirely Australian. Including subspecies and varieties, there are nearly one hundred different banksias in Australia, the majority coming from Western Australia. With few exceptions these inhabit poor sandy or gravelly soils in either forest, woodland, or inland sand heath. The majority do not reach tree size and are usually large bushy shrubs, but they also grade down to spreading prostrate species. Their usual flowering period is late summer through autumn and winter, when other flowers are scarce, although some are spring-flowering.

Giant Banksia is only a small tree, seldom exceeding about 8 m in height. In its young stages it grows very straight and upright, and with its large, deeply saw-toothed leaves and handsome soft woolly reddish-coloured new growth, it rather resembles a tropical hothouse plant. Eventually it forms a tree of fairly upright shape with rough grey bark, and sometimes with spreading limbs. The huge divided leaves, with a silvery reverse, form a circlet around the flower spikes which emerge in spring and summer, like large erect golden candles. These are followed by long fruiting cones with sharp seed follicles.

This tree is particularly ornamental, and can be grown in dense shade as well as in other conditions. Few of the western banksias, however, have yet proved reliable in cultivation, except in very well-drained light soils.

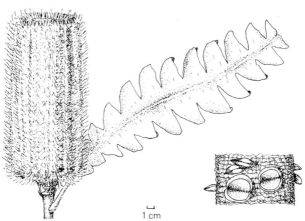

1 cm

COAST BANKSIA

Banksia integrifolia L. f.
PROTEACEAE

Of the eastern banksias, Coast Banksia is perhaps the best-known tree; it is often found inhabiting coastal sites along the sandy shores of many parts of Victoria, New South Wales, and Queensland. It sometimes extends further inland, and is found in mountainous country, often in a stunted, shrubby form.

This widespread species has been separated into several varieties by A. S. George (*Nuytsia*, vol. 3, no. 3, 1981, pp. 277–84).

Usually under 10 m, the tree, particularly in coastal situations, is most often gnarled and crooked or straggling, buffeted by strong sea winds. The irregular shapes so formed display a character and harsh beauty often associated with hard conditions. Coast Banksia has a rough light grey bark, and dark green, smooth-edged leaves with a silvery reverse, particularly striking in windy weather. The leaves are rounded at the tips and taper to a short stalk with a prominent midrib, 7–14 cm long by about 1 cm broad.

The pale yellow inflorescences are 6–12 cm long by about 5 cm in diameter, and occur in dense cylindrical spikes in autumn–winter.

The timber is soft and easily worked, and is occasionally used for small fancy woodwork.

Coast Banksia is an excellent tree for seaside conditions; it thrives in the acid, sandy soils of many parts of the eastern States, and is also a useful honey tree.

SILVER BANKSIA *B. marginata* Cav. is a similar tree but of more regular shape, often well branched to near ground level. It is widely distributed in the eucalypt forest areas of the eastern States and extends to the wetter parts of South Australia such as the Mount Lofty Ranges and the south-east, and to Tasmania.

A very rewarding sight in midwinter is this tree massed in flowers and seed cones and showing all the various flowering stages at the one time. When half-opened the spikes are slender and greenish; at maturity they are pale yellow; then they darken with age, until the very old spikes become grey although they still retain their characteristic shape; and finally come the fruiting cones.

This is a lovely tree, well worth cultivating, but it prefers adequate moisture and good drainage.

The remaining eastern banksias are mainly large shrubby species, although the common SAW BANKSIA *B. serrata* L. f. reaches tree proportions under favourable conditions.

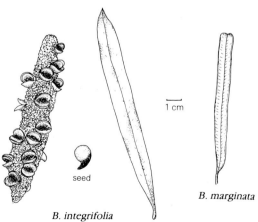

seed

B. integrifolia

1 cm

B. marginata

FIREWOOD BANKSIA, MENZIES' BANKSIA

Banksia menziesii R. Br.

PROTEACEAE

This banksia is a common tree in the Perth area but extends north to the Murchison River area and inland to the northern sand heaths of the Avon district of Western Australia.

The tree bears large, acorn-shaped flower spikes in autumn and winter, their beauty and rich colouring being typified in the photograph opposite. These occur in wine red and yellow forms, the styles being tipped with a long, golden, deeply furrowed pollen presenter. The seed cones which follow display a few prominent, scattered, furry seed capsules, protruding from a beautifully textured spike which resembles the weave in a grey and brown felted cloth.

The characteristic inflorescences of the genus are large, dense cylindrical spikes, sometimes more than 30 cm long and 7 cm or more in diameter; they usually sit upright on the branches. These spikes, which contain many individual flowers, form thick woody fruiting cones, each fruit (or follicle) in the cone containing two valves in which are two black, winged seeds. The fruits only open after extreme heat, and must be exposed to a flame, or allowed to remain in a hot oven for some time, before the seeds can be extracted.

Banksia trees, including Firewood Banksia, are rather crooked, with a bushy crown and a stout, gnarled stem covered with thick grey bark, and seldom exceed 10 m in height. The main differences are in the leaves, which are often large and deeply serrated, and, in some cases, in the inflorescences.

HOLLY-LEAVED BANKSIA *B. ilicifolia* R. Br. is a small tree 5–10 m high and often a companion of Firewood Banksia, but is found much further south, as far as the Albany area. It differs from most of the *Banksia* genus insofar as the flowers form a rounded rosette encircled by the leaves, rather than the usual spike. The tree is generally stiffer and more erect than other banksia trees.

MATCHSTICK BANKSIA *B. cuneata* A. S. George may reach 5 m high and has similar-shaped cream and pink flowers but smoother bark and smaller leaves than *B. ilicifolia*. It is an endangered species from the Quairading district, WA.

ORANGE BANKSIA *B. prionotes* Lindl. is another common tree of the south-west including the Perth area, particularly the northern districts, but it extends inland and further south than Firewood Banksia. It is noted for its large spectacular orange and woolly white flower spikes in late summer and autumn.

B. menziesii

1 cm

B. prionotes

B. ilicifolia

CROWN OF GOLD TREE

Barklya syringifolia F. Muell.

FABACEAE

The only member of its genus and limited to Australia, *Barklya syringifolia* is another one of the rainforest trees with spectacular flowers and one which, in a cultivated situation, forms only a small and colourful garden tree greatly admired for its ornamental value. It is cultivated in other countries, such as South Africa, France, Hawaii and the United States, where it is known as Golden Blossom Tree.

The tree is native to the rainforests of south-east Queensland and northern New South Wales but is not common. It can be found in the Albert River district south of Brisbane.

Crown of Gold Tree can reach about 18 m in the rainforest, but in cultivation it is slow-growing and is rarely seen taller than 7 m. It usually forms a dense-foliaged small tree with smooth, glossy, heart-shaped leaves of varying size, alternate or sometimes emanating in threes from the nodes, on stalks up to 7 cm long. The small five-petalled pea flowers are produced profusely in late spring and early summer, forming erect golden racemes held prominently above the foliage. Individual flowers are about 1 cm across and inflorescences are 8–12 cm long. The fruit is a small pod about 5 cm long with one or two seeds.

Barklya is easily propagated from either seed or cuttings and in cultivation is best suited to the warmer districts from Sydney to north Queensland and where moisture is assured. It is moderately frost-tolerant.

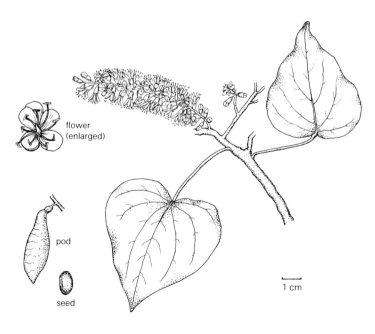

flower
(enlarged)

pod

seed

1 cm

FLAME TREE, ILLAWARRA FLAME TREE

Brachychiton acerifolius F. Muell.
STERCULIACEAE

At its best, the Flame Tree is one of Australia's most beautiful flowering trees, and it is extensively cultivated in Australia and overseas for ornamentation. It is an inhabitant of the sub-tropical brush forests from the Illawarra district in New South Wales to near Innisfail in Queensland.

Brachychiton species are mainly trees of the tropics where it is their habit to deciduate or partly deciduate following the 'dry' (winter), flower, and produce new foliage when the summer 'wet' begins. When planted in temperate climates of mainly winter rain, they retain this characteristic and still drop their leaves in late spring, prior to early summer flowering. They are typically pyramidal trees with a trunk which tapers from the base to a slender tip. Their seed is hairy or bristly and is contained in large boat-shaped follicles. When shed, the seeds leave an outer coat which forms a honeycomb structure within the follicles. The generic name is derived from this, *brachy* meaning short, and *chiton* a coat, referring to this loose outer covering of the seed. Many species are known as kurrajongs.

Flame Tree is naturally a large pyramidal tree to 40 m high, although it never attains this size when cultivated in the south. The large palmate leaves are glossy and variable, often deeply divided into 5–7 lobes. The brilliant scarlet, waxy bell flowers on scarlet stalks appear in November or December in numerous axillary clusters. In a good year these cover the whole tree after leaf fall, producing a glorious effect. The bristly seeds are bright yellow and are contained in follicles up to 10 cm long. Flame Tree is cultivated successfully as far south as Adelaide, but prefers fairly rich, moist soils.

Brachychiton species hybridise very freely, several hybrids of the above species being in cultivation.

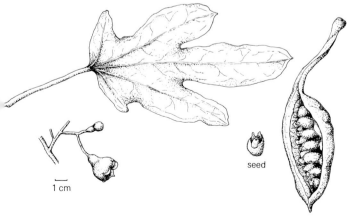

seed

|— 1 cm

LACEBARK TREE, SCRUB BOTTLE TREE, WHITE KURRAJONG

Brachychiton discolor F. Muell.

STERCULIACEAE

Another member of the kurrajong group which, at its best, displays flowers of great beauty.

Lacebark Tree is native to the near-coast brush forests and drier scrubs of northern New South Wales to Queensland as far as Maryborough and inland to the Bunya Mountains.

In rainforest it is a large, erect tree, more than 30 m high, with a thick, slightly bottle-shaped trunk and hard grey fissured or furrowed bark. In less favourable situations, however, such as in the drier scrubs and in cultivation, the tree is usually much smaller, 6–10 m high with a pyramidal or rounded canopy.

The leaves are broad and 3–7-lobed, on long petioles, with a downy undersurface. They are alternate, but clustered more densely towards the ends of the branches, and are of varying size, normally 10–15 cm broad and long. The immature leaves are more intricately lobed. Stalks, branchlets, seed pods and flowers as well as the undersurfaces of the leaves are covered with short downy hairs.

In early summer the tree deciduates and then produces its large, showy, bell-shaped flowers, 5–6 cm across, in thick clusters on the bare branches. These may be a deep reddish pink or a more delicate pale pink, but are always very ornamental. Trees do not necessarily flower well every year — it depends on the season.

Fruits are large, boat-shaped follicles, 7–12 cm long, on stalks about 2 cm long, containing bristly seeds, similar to those of other *Brachychiton* species. Lacebark Tree is relatively hardy in cultivation and is successful in areas of cold winters such as Adelaide, where it has succeeded on a range of soils, including limestone.

There are several undescribed species which are similar, but usually smaller, deciduous trees, from the dry scrubs of the tropical north, particularly the Northern Territory, and which have horticultural potential because of their large, colourful flowers.

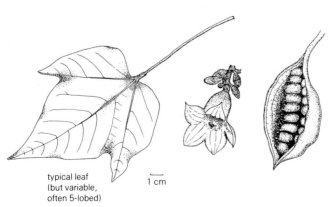

typical leaf
(but variable,
often 5-lobed)

1 cm

KURRAJONG, BLACK KURRAJONG

Brachychiton populneus (Schott & Endl.) R. Br.
STERCULIACEAE

Kurrajong is a commonly cultivated versatile tree which is naturally widely distributed in eastern Australia. It occurs from inland and southern Queensland throughout New South Wales, but particularly on the western slopes and plains, and in east and north-east Victoria. The tree is found on a variety of soils, but often shows a preference for those of limestone origin.

The name Kurrajong originated from an Aboriginal word *currajong* meaning 'fibre-yielding plant', the bark fibres being used by Aboriginals for making nets.

The tree is densely foliaged, and of moderate to large size, usually 14–20 m high, with a stout, grey-barked trunk. In its early stages it grows pyramidal with a green bark, but in time it develops a spreading crown which gives dense shade. The glossy dark green leaves occur on long stalks (petioles), and are very variable in shape, from entire and poplar-like to partly divided or deeply lobed. When young they are pale green, almost chartreuse in colour, the whole tree having this appearance when producing its new foliage.

The small bell-shaped flowers borne in axillary panicles are cream or greenish, with red, yellow, or purplish-coloured throats. The seed follicles are about 8 cm long, and the seeds black and numerous. Flowering is variable, usually March to early summer.

Kurrajong is an extremely valuable tree, adaptable to varied soils, deep-rooted, and excellent for ornament, shade, and shelter, as well as a good fodder tree in times of drought. Its virtues are appreciated by landowners who now preserve it, particularly in the drier areas of its range.

DESERT KURRAJONG *B. gregorii* F. Muell. is a smaller dry area species belonging to the same group and superficially often resembling a poor specimen of Kurrajong. The leaves have 3–5 linear-lanceolate lobes, and the seed follicles are smaller than those of the Kurrajong, with fewer seeds in each. Flowers are pale yellow. This tree is found in arid parts from the Murchison River in Western Australia to north of Kalgoorlie, thence across the Victoria Desert to the region of the Musgrave, Birksgate, and Mann Ranges in South and Western Australia.

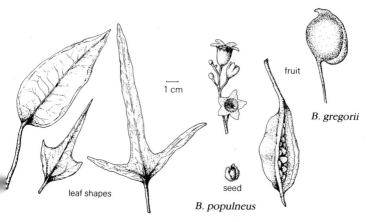

leaf shapes

1 cm

B. populneus

seed

fruit

B. gregorii

HYBRID FLAME TREE

Brachychiton populneus × *acerifolius*
STERCULIACEAE

Sometimes referred to as *Brachychiton hybrida*, this beautiful flowering tree is a naturally occurring but variable hybrid between the Illawarra Flame Tree (*B. acerifolius*, see p. 78) and the Kurrajong (*B. populneus*, p. 82). Although perhaps not as spectacular as the vivid red of a good form of the Illawarra Flame Tree in full flower, at its best this tree gives the impression of a pinkish red cloud when seen from a distance, this feature being evident in the photograph opposite. A large tree in full bloom, usually during November–December, is a magnificent sight.

In size and habit the tree resembles the common Kurrajong, often being pyramidal and densely branched with a stout, erect trunk. About 14 m appears to be its maximum height. It features characteristics of both parent trees, the large leaves being variable, rarely as deeply lobed as in the Flame Tree, and when entire similar to those of the Kurrajong. Apart from their much paler colour, the trusses of bell-shaped flowers are just as numerous and conspicuous as their counterparts on the Flame Tree. The large boat-shaped seed pods too, are difficult to distinguish from those of the parents. Bark is slightly rough and dark grey.

This is a hardy, easily cultivated tree, which partly deciduates in late spring before flowering. In cooler areas such as Adelaide and Melbourne it is fairly slow growing, at least during its early years.

QUEENSLAND BOTTLE TREE *Brachychiton rupestre* (Lindl.) K. Schum. This easily recognised tree of the *Brachychiton* genus is native to mainly the drier scrubs of central Queensland, where it is conspicuous because of its thick, bottle-shaped trunk. Typical of the genus, it has variable, lobed juvenile leaves but entire and narrow mature leaves. Fruiting follicles are more rounded than those of the Kurrajong, with a prominent beak. The tree is sometimes cultivated and can be seen in Brisbane parks.

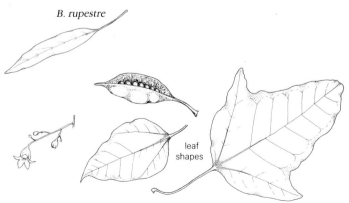

B. rupestre

leaf
shapes

1 cm

BUCKINGHAMIA, IVORY CURL FLOWER

Buckinghamia celsissima F. Muell.

PROTEACEAE

This is a northern rainforest tree from the Atherton Tableland and adjacent areas and is the only *Buckinghamia* species endemic to Australia.

Buckinghamia is distinguished by the pedicels of each flower arising directly from the rachis, and by its four ovules and seeds.

Despite its rather restricted habitat, it is fairly well known because of its popularity as a cultivated tree, particularly along the warm east coast. This is due to its profuse flowering and its adaptability to a range of conditions, as well as its growth habit, which lends it to street planting as well as other situations.

In the rainforest the tree can reach 25 m high, but in cultivation it develops a dense, rounded, bushy crown and 6–8 m appears to be about its limit. It is fast growing when young, but at maturity its growth appears to go into leaf and flower production rather than extending its branches.

The very variable leathery leaves are smooth, a deep glossy green, sometimes silvery beneath, and either entire or variously lobed. The showy cream-coloured inflorescences are prolific, covering the tree for about 4 weeks in summer (January–February) in racemes up to 22 cm long of sweetly perfumed, honey-laden flowers which are loved by bees. These are followed by grevillea-like follicles, up to 1·5 cm long, containing 1–4 flat, papery seeds, from which young trees can easily be propagated.

Seedling trees seem to be very consistent in growth habit and flower production, adding to the other excellent features of this tree for garden culture.

Athough preferring good soil it adapts well to other soil types and is known to have been grown successfully as far south as Melbourne. It is an easily managed tree in cultivation, seldom requiring more than a light trim after flowering, and sometimes flowering twice a year (summer and winter, in Adelaide).

In many respects it resembles the White Silky Oak (*Grevillea hilliana*, see p.220), and it is sometimes mistaken for that tree.

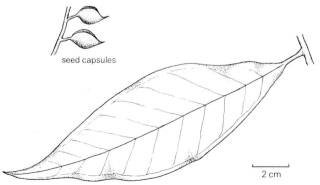

seed capsules

2 cm

NATIVE BOX, SWEET BURSARIA, CHRISTMAS BUSH

Bursaria spinosa Cav.
PITTOSPORACEAE

Native Box is a widespread species found throughout temperate Australia. It occurs on many different soil types and in many environments, often as quite a small shrub to only about 2 m high, but in other situations as a small, rather spreading tree to 7–10 m high. In the south-east of South Australia it forms quite a handsome tree, particularly along the coast.

The common name of Native Box was originated by the early settlers because of the resemblance of the leaves to the common English Box Tree.

The tree is only short-trunked, often crooked, with a very rugged dark grey bark and small thorns or spines on the branchlets. The leaves are scattered and very variable, entire, and usually obovate or ovate-lanceolate in shape. They are glabrous and bright green on both sides with a prominent midrib.

About Christmas time or later the plant flowers, producing an abundance of small, sweetly scented, white or cream star-shaped blossoms. These are borne above the foliage in dense, upright panicles which make a fine show, and attract bees in large swarms.

The small, brown purse-like or pouched seed vessels that follow give to the plant its generic name of *Bursaria*, from the Latin word for purse.

Native Box is seldom seen in cultivation, but should receive more attention as an ornamental small flowering tree or shrub. It will grow in most soils and situations but is more likely to reach tree size where moisture is abundant. When kept to shrubby proportions it makes quite an attractive and useful hedge plant.

There are only three Australian species of *Bursaria*.

BOX OLIVE WOOD *B. incana* Lindl. is a small, erect tree from southern Queensland with small leaves which are hoary underneath, and terminal panicles of white flowers.

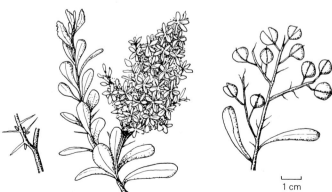

1 cm

WHITE BOTTLEBRUSH

Callistemon salignus (Smith) DC.
MYRTACEAE

White Bottlebrush is only a small tree, sometimes a shrub, which is widely distributed throughout temperate Australia in forest country extending from Queensland as far north as Bundaberg to the Torrens George near Adelaide in South Australia. Different forms of the species can be found within this range.

This is a tree member of the well-known bottlebrush group consisting mainly of large shrubs which are commonly cultivated both in Australia and overseas, and prized for the beauty of their large, spectacular flowers.

Callistemons are characterised by these conspicuous and stalkless (sessile) flowers which consist mainly of numerous long stamens, usually a vivid red, but sometimes cream, greenish yellow, or pink. The flower stamens are separated or free, which distinguishes *Callistemon* from the genus *Melaleuca* whose stamens are joined or united in bundles. The dense flower heads are prolific in spring, and are sometimes followed by a lesser flowering about autumn.

The flowers are followed by hard, woody seed capsules which encircle the stem in a close cylindrical group, and take about 3 years to mature. The minute seeds remain viable for many years until fire or some other agent allows the fruits to open.

White Bottlebrush is usually a bushy-crowned tree up to 10 m in height. The trunk is slender with a whitish papery bark. The narrow, pointed leaves are shining and willowy, 5–10 cm long by about 1 cm broad, with a distinct midrib, their most striking feature being the bright pink to red colour of the new growing tips. These are soft and downy and make a display as attractive as the flowers.

The flowers are usually a creamy white colour, although pink and red colour forms occur. Fruits are rounded, about 3 mm in diameter.

This is a useful tree for beekeepers as it helps to build up nectar and pollen supplies in the spring for bee colonies. Being adaptable it is also valued as an ornamental tree, although it prefers non-limestone moist soils. It flowers at the same time as the Weeping Bottlebrush (see p. 92), and, planted together, the two make a spectacular display of red and white blossoms.

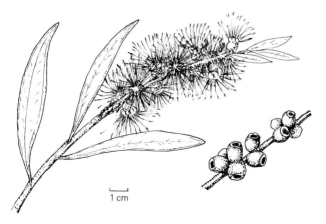

1 cm

WEEPING BOTTLEBRUSH

Callistemon viminalis G. Don ex Loud.
MYRTACEAE

Weeping Bottlebrush is a commonly cultivated tree naturally found growing mainly along the banks of rivers and creeks throughout eastern Queensland and north-eastern New South Wales north of the Hunter River. In some parts it extends into the higher tablelands.

This tree is the largest member of the bottlebrush genus, sometimes reaching 20 m in height, although usually under 10 m. The common name 'bottlebrush' is reserved for members of the *Callistemon* genus, although several other Australian plants such as some *Melaleuca* and *Banksia* species also have flowers of this shape.

The Weeping Bottlebrush is often scraggy when seen growing naturally, but usually forms a neat, willowy tree with long, slender and drooping smaller branches when cultivated. The trunk is slender, and the bark rough, dark grey, and furrowed. The long narrow leaves (about 7 cm long by 6 mm broad) have a prominent midrib, and are tapered at each end on very short stalks. When crushed they emit a pleasant myrtle scent.

The colour of the leaves varies as they age. The very new tips are a bright, bronzy red, and are soft and downy in texture. As they develop they change to a soft pale green and eventually mature to a more rigid darker green, the whole effect being very attractive.

The flowers appear in spring in dense red spikes that cover the whole tree in a blaze of colour. Irregular flowering occurs at other times of the year also. Flowers are variable in both size and form. Good flowering forms should be reproduced by cuttings, which strike quite readily, rather than by seedlings, which are often disappointing.

The hard, woody fruits are cup-shaped, about 5 mm by 5 mm. This tree is also a valuable producer of nectar and pollen for bee colonies. It is valued as an ornamental tree and is easily grown, preferring non-limestone soils with adequate moisture supplies. Under these conditions growth is quite rapid. It is also useful as a street tree where rainfall exceeds 400 mm annually.

stamens

1 cm

WHITE CYPRESS PINE

Callitris columellaris F. Muell.
CUPRESSACEAE

The *Callitris* species or native cypress pines are an ornamental and important group of conifers found throughout Australia, very often forming pure stands in moderately dry localities, particularly where there are sandy soils.

White Cypress Pine is a particularly widespread species and is found in all mainland States, though mainly on the east coast and the western plains and slopes of New South Wales, and in south-east Queensland. In South Australia it is prevalent in the scenic Flinders Ranges where it is sometimes the dominant tree on rocky slopes and rises, and enhances the landscape.

White Cypress Pine favours a warm temperate inland climate with rainfall in the 400–750 mm range, although this is considerably higher in parts of the east coast, where climate is subtropical. It sometimes forms pure stands, but more often mixes with *Eucalyptus* species, usually on sandy or loamy soils.

The genus is distinguished by the tiny scale-like leaves in whorls of three or four along the branchlets, and by the fruiting cones with six woody scales, three being distinctly smaller than the others. These contain hard, winged seeds which germinate very freely.

This particular species is a large, fastigiate tree, 20–30 m high at its best, but considerably smaller in some of its habitat localities. The bark is dark grey, rough, and furrowed, and persists to the smaller branches; the foliage is often glaucous. The 'flowers' are not conspicuous, and are unisexual conelets or catkins. Fruits are dark brown and spherical, about 2 cm or less in diameter.

The softwood timber of this tree is renowned for its resistance to termite attack and is used extensively in the building trade.

There are several other species of native cypress pines, which are all ornamental, particularly when grown in clumps of three or four together. They should be more widely grown as garden trees.

seed

1 cm

BLACK CYPRESS PINE, MURRAY PINE

Callitris preissii Miq.
CUPRESSACEAE

This is another widespread species of native pine with foliage similar to that of the White Cypress Pine (p.94) but usually of a much brighter emerald green. In South Australia it is found on Kangaroo Island, Eyre Peninsula, the Flinders Ranges (where not as prevalent as *C. columellaris*), the Murray Mallee and the upper south-east, as well as the Adelaide area where good specimens can still be seen, particularly on some of the western golf courses. It is also fairly common in the drier parts of western Victoria and New South Wales, particularly along the River Murray and the adjacent mallee country.

Black Cypress Pine favours sandy soils but is not confined to these. At its best it reaches a height of about 15 m with an upright habit. However, in the poorer soils and drier conditions encountered within its habitat range, it grows much smaller and bushier.

The scale-like leaves are arranged in groups of three around the branchlets. The 'flowers', also, are similar to those of White Cypress Pine, with separate female and male 'flowers' on each tree. The female conelets or catkins comprise six scales and are slightly larger than those of the pollen-producing male conelets.

It is the larger fruiting cones which readily distinguish this tree from the White Cypress Pine. These are up to 3 cm long by 2–2·5 cm wide before opening, with a smooth outer surface when green but prominently wrinkled when dry. They open into six sharp-pointed valves containing hard, winged seeds which germinate freely.

The brown timber has a compact grain and a refreshing pine-like odour. It is just as termite-resistant as that of the White Cypress Pine.

C. preissii Miq. subsp. *verrucosa* (A. Cunn. ex Endl.) J. Garden is a bushier tree or large shrub to 3 m high which favours sand dunes. It is found in all mainland States except Queensland but is not as widespread as the preceding species, and is distinguished by the prominent rounded warts on the fruiting cones.

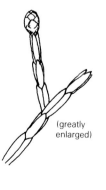

(greatly
enlarged)

1 cm

BEAUTY LEAF, BEACH CALOPHYLLUM, MASTWOOD, ALEXANDRIAN LAUREL

Calophyllum inophyllum L.
CLUSIACEAE

This is a common tree of the coastal rainforest dunes of north-east Australia, where its massive roots can be found anchoring the tree and stabilising the shoreline. It is also native to India and Malaya. Like other trees of this habitat, it is inclined to lean towards the sea, and is often seen growing from old trunks and branches which have re-rooted themselves after falling from parent trees. It also germinates freely from the fallen fruit, but is slow growing.

Superficially, the tree resembles the figs (*Ficus*) with its short, thick trunk, or sometimes several trunks emanating from the spreading roots, and wide-spreading branches, the tree's width usually being equal to its height of 10–12 m in mature specimens.

The leaves, too, are thick and fig-like, smooth, with a prominent midrib, and arranged in opposite pairs. They are oval, normally about 12–15 cm long by 6–8 cm wide with numerous, closely and evenly spaced, parallel, faint lateral veins. The persistent bark is hard, dark grey and furrowed, providing an excellent home for epiphytes.

The distinguishing feature of the tree is its large, globular, green fruits, 3–4 cm in diameter, which are borne prominently in clusters on long, pendulous stalks. These turn blue as they ripen, and then brown after falling, wrinkling to resemble a fallen walnut. The kernel is soft, about 2·5 cm in diameter and roughly heart-shaped.

Flowers are white and fragrant, not spectacular, but attractive, appearing in short axillary racemes, each flower 2–2·5 cm across, with four petals, bright yellow, brown-tipped stamens, and four cup-shaped white bracteoles. Flowering is mainly in summer but may occur at any time.

This is a fine tree for coastal planting in the warmer tropical to subtropical regions of Australia, where it provides ample shade and shelter from the sun and protection against coastal erosion. It is sometimes used as a formal park specimen tree and a few such examples can be found in Cairns.

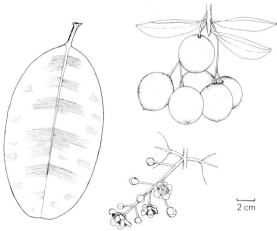

2 cm

NATIVE or WILD ORANGE

Capparis mitchellii Lindl.
CAPPARACEAE

Commemorating with its botanical name its discoverer, Sir Thomas Mitchell, Native Orange is only a small tree from the arid inland. It is found in the far north of South Australia, mainly in the Cooper's Creek–Lake Frome area, in central Australia, and in the dry parts of New South Wales, Queensland, and Victoria, usually on clay or loamy soils. It is protected by law in South Australia.

In its early stages the plant is only a scrambly, prickly shrub, but it soon develops a more sturdy habit, and eventually forms a rather compact tree, often with several joined main stems. It is not a plant to go unnoticed with its dense habit and deep, sombre, green foliage, giving it a solid, permanent appearance as though it could withstand any adverse condition it might encounter.

The branches of this small and compact tree, which grows to about 7–8 cm, sometimes reach to near the ground. Often it is wider in girth than it is high. Leaves are broadly lance-shaped or ovate, about 5 cm long, and rather rough in texture, being clothed with a short, dense tomentum. The showy flowers, up to 6 cm across, are white or cream in colour, and are produced freely from September to November, though each flower only lasts one day. Each flower consists of a bunch of about 50 long stamens in the centre of several rather broad petals. The solitary fruit, produced on a long stem, is about the size of a golf ball. It is deep green, hard, and woody, and contains large flat seeds. At one time they were occasionally eaten by Aboriginals, but they are not generally considered edible.

Native Orange is a very useful tree in the interior in that it provides shade and shelter for stock. It has been successfully cultivated in Adelaide and warrants consideration for garden culture, particularly in dry areas.

Capparis is a large genus of plants found in warm climates throughout the world. There are a number of other Australian species but these are shrubs or climbing plants, mostly native to Queensland.

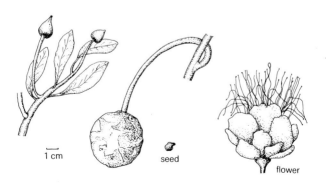

1 cm

seed

flower

NORTHERN SILKY OAK

Cardwellia sublimis F. Muell.

PROTEACEAE

This rainforest tree from northern Queensland is very easily identified by its large and conspicuous, oval greyish fruits, up to about 12 cm long, which are borne prominently above the foliage. A close look at the photograph will show the reader the characteristic fruit arrangement. If the fruits are not present on the tree there are usually some empty husks on the ground beneath it to aid identification.

Northern Silky Oak has a fairly restricted habitat range from near Townsville to Bloomfield. Within its range, however, it is quite common, and can be found in many rainforest associations and on a variety of soil types. It is the only known species of *Cardwellia.*

Within natural forest the tree is tall and erect, to 40 m high, seldom buttressed at the base, and with a light canopy of foliage above its long, normally straight, bole. Some trees are occasionally encountered on cleared farmland, however, and these also grow erect but are generally much smaller, with a narrow branching habit over most of the trunk. The bark is brown, slightly rough and flaky.

The leaves are pinnate, deep green and smooth above but often with silky brownish hairs on the undersurface. Leaflets are prominently veined, oblong to ovate, about 8–18 cm long by 3–7 cm broad, arranged in opposite pairs with no terminal leaflet present. New growth is a silky golden brown or pinkish colour.

Racemes of attractive creamy white flowers, each raceme about 12 cm long, are borne freely from October to December and make a fine show. The flowers are arranged in opposite pairs.

The fruits are large, woody follicles as described earlier and contain flat brown winged seeds about 7 cm long by 3 cm wide, which may retain their viability for up to 2 years.

Northern Silky Oak was the most important tree of the north Queensland timber industry in 1985, comprising up to 15% of its total mill intake. It is a decorative and durable timber for inside construction and furniture.

Although seldom cultivated, it would be an ornamental medium-sized tree for tropical gardens with an acid, well-drained soil. The author has no knowledge of its potential in colder climates.

fruit

flower buds

1 cm

opened fruit husk without seeds

BLACK BEAN,
MORETON BAY CHESTNUT

Castanospermum australe Cunn. ex C. Fraser ex Hook.
FABACEAE

Black Bean is a tree of the brush forests of northern New South
Wales and Queensland, where it extends as far north as Cape
York Peninsula and inland some 150 km from the coast. It
favours good, rich, moist soils following watercourses.

The tree is an ornamental one, as well as a much sought-after
timber tree. In its natural environment it can reach a height of
40 m, but under cultivation, particularly in the cooler southern
temperate locations such as Adelaide and Melbourne where it
is successfully cultivated, it seldom exceeds 8–14 m. Here it
sometimes forms a dense shade tree with several main stems.

Bark is slightly rough, grey or brown in colour, and the foliage is dark green and glossy, and handsome at all times. Leaves
are long (up to 50 cm) and divided into a number of leaflets
(pinnate), giving a frond-like appearance. Each leaf consists of
8–17 alternate leaflets, 5–12 cm long, and narrowly elliptical or
oval in shape.

The flowers, which bloom in October–November on the previous season's wood, are pea-like and individually large (up to
4 cm long), and appear in showy racemes; they are usually a
deep golden orange in colour. The flowers are sometimes
sparse, and in any case can be partly hidden by the dense
foliage.

The seeds are contained in large, heavy brown pods up to
25 cm long, and are themselves large and brown, about the size
of a large chestnut. When green they are poisonous.

The attractive, dark brown timber is hard and heavy, polishes
and dresses well, and is prized for fancy woodwork and
furniture, having a teak-like appearance.

Black Bean makes an excellent shade and shelter tree on
cleared land and has sometimes been preserved for this purpose. It grows successfully in climates colder than in its natural
environment, but should be grown on the moist, higher-grade
soils of these areas. It is used also as a container plant.

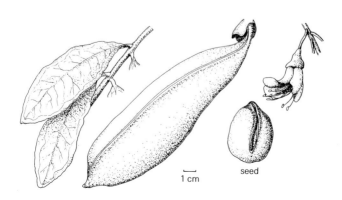

1 cm

seed

BLACK OAK, BELAH

Casuarina cristata Miq. ssp. *pauper*
(F. Muell. ex Miq.) L. Johnson
CASUARINACEAE

Occurring in all mainland States, Black Oak is one of the most common members of the casuarina family, a large and interesting group of Australian trees and shrubs commonly known as 'oaks' or 'she-oaks'. They all feature certain characteristics which are described on page 108 under *C. cunninghamiana*.

The casuarina family was revised in 1982, the revision including the separation of *Casuarina* into two genera — *Allocasuarina* and *Casuarina* (see p. 42 under *A. decaisneana*).

Black Oak is mainly a tree of the arid and harsh conditions of the outback, where it is often the dominant woodland species. Here it usually appears as a drab, sombre tree of small proportions, rarely more than 7–8 m high and often poorly branched, as it struggles for survival on shallow limestone soils. At its best, however, or where water is available, Black Oak grows to a fine tree to 15 m high, suitable for farm or ornamental planting on most soils. In South Australia it extends into the northern wheatlands where rainfall averages about 450 mm annually.

The leaves are minute scales or teeth at each junction of the soft, segmented branchlets (cladodes). The unisexual flowers are usually on separate trees, appearing in summer. Female flowers are concentrated into a head attached directly to one of the smaller branches, while the male flowers form segmented spikes at the ends of the branchlets and give a brownish colour to the tree in flower.

The woody seed cones are produced on the female trees only and are 1·5–3 cm long by about 1·5–2 cm across. They are more or less barrel-shaped and contain small winged seeds.

The common name refers to the tree's dark grey or black, rough, persistent bark and the similarity of the figured timber to that of Northern Hemisphere oaks (*Quercus*). Timber is durable and a good fuel.

Casuarina cristata Miq. ssp. *cristata* L. Johnson, also known as Black Oak, allegedly occurs only in Queensland and New South Wales, where it is less common than the subspecies *pauper*.

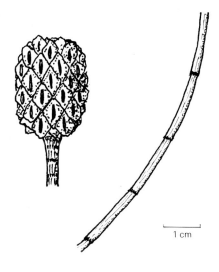

1 cm

RIVER OAK

Casuarina cunninghamiana Miq.
CASUARINACEAE

Perhaps the largest tree of the casuarina family, River Oak portrays the peculiar characteristics of this interesting family (including *Allocasuarina* — see pp.42–49) very well.

These include long, needle-like green cladodes which act as leaves but are really small branches. The true leaves are tiny tooth-like scales which encircle the joints of these cladodes at regular intervals. The male and female flowers occur on separate trees and appear in a different manner on each. On the female trees they are small, red-coloured, cone-shaped, and attached to the main branchlets by a short stalk; they are followed by woody cones containing the fruit. The male flowers appear as small terminal spikes at the ends of the cladodes; they are often golden brown or red in colour, and so abundant that they create a very beautiful effect.

River Oak is a natural inhabitant of the margins of freshwater rivers and streams in the relatively high rainfall country (500 to over 1500 mm) of New South Wales, Queensland, and Arnhem Land as far as the Daly River. Over this range conditions vary from dry temperate, where frosts are quite severe, to tropical, where frosts are nil. At all times its need of water other than natural rainfall is apparent. Soils are usually alluvial loams or sands.

The tree is large, majestic, and usually pyramidal, 15–35 m high, with an upright trunk. The branches are fairly densely clothed, horizontal to semi-pendulous, sometimes occurring near ground level; foliage is a lustrous green and pine-like. The bark on the trunk and main limbs is rough, deeply furrowed, and dark grey in colour.

River Oak is an ornamental species good for cultivation, adaptable to soil differences, and able to tolerate rainfall as low as 375 mm. It flowers from April to October.

SWAMP OAK *C. glauca* Sieb. Robust and erect, this is a somewhat similar but more sombre tree, native to the brackish lagoons and tidal rivers of east and south-east Australia. It is widely planted on account of its ability to flourish under harsh conditions on practically any soil including saline. It suckers freely and forms a good windbreak.

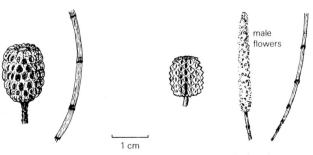

C. glauca   *C. cunninghamiana*

male
flowers

1 cm

SHINGLE OAK, HORSETAIL SHE-OAK

Casuarina equisetifolia Forst. & Forst. f.
ssp. *incana* (Benth.) L. Johnson
CASUARINACEAE

This lovely tree can be seen along the sea coast of north-eastern Australia, where it is a common tree in northern New South Wales and Queensland. It grows right to the water's edge and its graceful, drooping foliage enhances many a scenic seascape. Because of its tolerance to sea winds and its ornamental appearance, it is now extensively cultivated in the warmer coastal regions of Australia.

The tree is usually only small, seldom more than 6–7 m high, with a rounded, pendulous crown. In some parts of its range, however, it grows much taller. Bark on the trunk and larger branches is a polished brown-grey. This is topped by narrow, weeping foliage which shimmers like silver in sunlight — an effect due, no doubt, to the whitish ends to the grey-green branchlets.

As in all *Casuarina* and *Allocasuarina* species, the leaves are represented by a ring of small, scale-like teeth around the branchlets. Flowers are unisexual, the male and female flowers appearing on separate trees. The woody seed cones are relatively small, about 2 cm across and broadly barrel-shaped.

This tree is important because of its ability to stabilise coastal sand dunes. For this reason, and because of its ornamental appearance, it is widely used by councils and beach protection authorities along the warmer east coast regions of Australia.

Although not an easy species to grow elsewhere, it readily adapts in coastal sands where it is easily propagated, large cuttings being able to be struck in situ where the tree is to be established. Propagation by seed is also very easy.

Casuarina equisetifolia Forst. & Forst. f. ssp. *equisetifolia* also occurs in Australia near Darwin, but is more prevalent in the islands of the Pacific.

seed

1 cm

COACHWOOD, SCENTED SATINWOOD

Ceratopetalum apetalum D. Don
CUNONIACEAE

Coachwood is one of the most important timber trees of the New South Wales coastal brush forests, where it occurs from Batemans Bay in the south to as far north as the Macpherson Range near the Queensland border.

The genus *Ceratopetalum* comprises six described species, of which only one, *C. succirubrum*, is found away from the tropical or subtropical east coast of Australia: this species occurs also in New Guinea. The genus is characterised by the toothed leaves which are opposite with one to three leaflets, and the four or five calyx segments with twice this number of stamens. Fruits are small and hard and surrounded by horizontal wing-like calyx lobes which turn bright red in some species.

Coachwood is a tall, shaft-like forest tree to 35 m high and has a trunk up to 1 m in diameter with a rough bark. The bark and wood are fragrant, owing apparently to the presence of the substance coumarin. The leaves are usually solitary, lanceolate or elliptical, and up to 13 cm long. The flowers have no petals, but the calyx lobes enlarge and turn a bright reddish colour, giving the tree colour in early summer.

The pale pink timber is light, strong, and easily worked. It is used extensively for furniture and interior woodwork.

This is an ornamental tree for moist, sheltered situations.

NEW SOUTH WALES CHRISTMAS BUSH *C. gummiferum* Sm. is the species best known in cultivation. It is native to northern and central coastal New South Wales, usually on sandstone where it is often only shrubby, but sometimes reaches tree proportions. It is the only species with petals. These are small, jagged, and white, and soon fall, leaving numerous calyx lobes which swell and turn a bright red or pink about Christmas time, when they make a spectacular display. The leaves are shining and three-lobed.

This species is very ornamental, but not easy to cultivate except in conditions akin to its natural environment.

Of the other four species, *C. virchowii* F. Muell., *C. corymbosum* C. T. White, and *C. succirubrum* C. T. White are all tall timber trees found in the Atherton Tableland region of northern Queensland, whilst *C. macrophyllum* Hoogl. is a recently described species from north Queensland (1984).

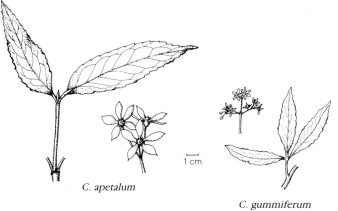

C. apetalum

1 cm

C. gummiferum

NATIVE POPLAR

Codonocarpus pyramidalis F. Muell.
GYROSTEMONACEAE

A very attractive, upright tree· endemic in South Australia, Native Poplar is found in the northern part of the State, mainly in the northern Flinders Range area.

The genus, consisting of only three species, is confined to Australia.

Native Poplar is a slender, upright tree to 8 m high, with a light fawn or brownish smooth trunk, and elegant, drooping branches. Where it grows it is an unusual and conspicuous feature of the vegetation, particularly when seen as isolated specimens in open, flat country. Foliage is bright green with leaves 5–10 cm long, very narrow, and rather soft and smooth in texture.

The flowers are fairly insignificant, but are followed by bell-shaped fruits, produced in dense clusters usually near the top of the tree. These are about 1 cm long, greenish yellow in colour, and very decorative. They usually occur in summer, but this varies.

It is doubtful if this tree has ever been cultivated. If tamed, especially in dry areas, it could become a popular and handsome subject for garden use.

C. cotinifolius (Desf.) F. Muell. is a related species also known as Native Poplar. This species is a slender, upright, and graceful tree 7–14 m in height, inhabiting the dry areas of all mainland States and often seen in pure stands.

The leaves are broader than in the preceding species and a bluish green in colour. The name Horse-radish Tree or sometimes Mustard Tree originated from the taste of these leaves. A medicinal product with a peculiar bitter taste comes from the bark, and the timber, although soft, is insect-resistant and useful.

The remaining species, *C. australis* Cunn., known as Bell Fruit Tree, is a similar, handsome tree to 8 m high, but with bright green, willow-like leaves. It is native only to New South Wales and Queensland.

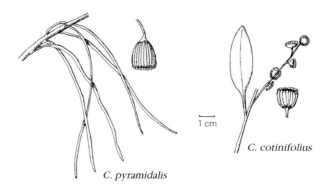

C. pyramidalis   1 cm   C. cotinifolius

CUPANIA

Cupaniopsis anacardioides (A. Rich.) Radlk.
SAPINDACEAE

Cupania is a dense evergreen tree native to the east coast of Australia from north of Sydney to Townsville in Queensland. It is very often found growing in coastal sands in isolated patches, and will withstand a certain amount of exposure to salt-laden winds, although too much exposure results in 'burning-off' on the windward side.

The tree resembles the cashew tree (*Anacardium*), from which it derives its specific epithet.

Cupania is not a tall tree, usually growing no higher than 8 m but sometimes reaching 14 m. Its spread nearly always exceeds its height and this habit together with its dense foliage makes it an ideal shade or street tree. The leaves are pinnate, consisting of 2–12 leaflets, dark green and shining. The small greyish white flowers occur in axillary or terminal panicles, but are insignificant. During November and December the numerous bright orange-red or yellow, small pumpkin-like fruits of this tree can make a most attractive display. Unfortunately only a small percentage of Cupanias possess this fruiting habit and the tree should be vegetatively propagated from good fruiting specimens.

This tree has received considerable attention as a street tree, particularly along the east coast, where it can be seen lining streets in towns from Newcastle to Rockhampton. Its wide-branching and low-growing habit makes it ideal to plant beneath overhead service wires to provide dense shade on hot summer days. It is versatile as regards soils, and will withstand strong winds very well. Cupania is cultivated as far south as Adelaide in South Australia, where it forms a neat tree to 8 m high.

There are several other species of *Cupaniopsis* native to the east coast but they are not commonly encountered or cultivated.

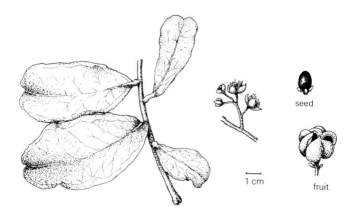

seed

fruit

1 cm

RED BEECH, GOLDEN GUINEA TREE

Dillenia alata Banks ex DC.
DILLENIACEAE

Usually only a small to medium-sized, erect tree, Red Beech is
native to tropical north Queensland and the Northern Territory,
where it is abundant in sandy, swampy depressions near and on
the coast. It is difficult to isolate trees because of associated
vines and other vegetation which often surround them and the
photograph, taken on the Cairns foreshore, perhaps does not
typify the tree in nature. Red Beech features a dense canopy of
glossy green foliage, the leaves being large and shiny, oval and,
on average, about 20 cm long by 12 cm wide, but sometimes
much larger, with conspicuously winged petioles (hence the
name *alata*) and prominent venation. Young leaves are yellow
to reddish brown in colour and old leaves turn yellow before
falling.

Flowers are bright yellow, 6–9 cm across, with four delicate,
fringed petals, which open fully and fall at a touch. These frame
a carmine red centre, the colour being due to numerous
recurved styles arising from many yellow stamens. The flowers
occur on long petioles, usually in twos. Each flower only lasts
1 day but they are borne over a long period, mainly during
winter (June–July). The flower buds resemble young green figs,
but have long stems. Fruits can occur at the same time as the
flowers and these are just as attractive when they ripen and
open to reveal usually seven boat-shaped, bright crimson segments surrounded by smooth green cup-shaped bracteoles.
There are usually one to three seeds per segment, each seed
surrounded by a soft, pulpy white aril. The hard brown seeds
resemble grape pips. The canopy of foliage often extends to
near the ground, hiding the tree's very ornamental, papery
bark, which is an attractive coppery pink, ageing to plum or
maroon in colour. This is a lovely tree inside its canopy and
should be cultivated more than it is as a small shade tree. The
lovely bark is an excellent support for epiphytes.

Red Beech is an ornamental small tree for wet, tropical
situations, particularly near coastal foreshores. It can be
found in many such situations from south of Cardwell to Cape
Tribulation in Queensland.

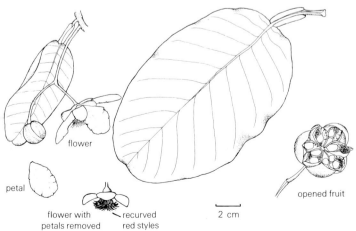

petal

flower

flower with petals removed — recurved red styles

opened fruit

2 cm

NATIVE TAMARIND

Diploglottis cunninghamii (Hook.) Hook. f.
syn. *Diploglottis australis* (G. Don) Radlk.
SAPINDACEAE

Native to the coastal scrubs or rainforests which extend from Illawarra in New South Wales to Townsville in Queensland, Native Tamarind is a very distinctive, easily recognised tree because of its foliage. It can readily be identified in the small remnant pockets of forest which are occasionally encountered, or, sometimes, as isolated specimens in the rural landscape. Although it may reach 30 m in its rainforest habitat, with a long straight bole about 150 cm in diameter, it is usually fairly small and slender when seen in isolation. A fine specimen can be seen in the Lions park just out of Lismore, NSW.

The genus is distinguished by its one-sided, incomplete disc on the fruit and its large leaflets which are usually more than 10 cm long. Native Tamarind is a handsome evergreen tree with slightly rough grey-brown bark. The leaves are very large and pinnate with each leaflet 8–25 cm long by 10 cm or more broad. The leaflets are wavy, with characteristic indentations across the surface, a bright shiny green on the upper side but dull and covered with rusty, velvety hairs beneath. These hairs extend to the young branches. The apex of each narrow elliptical leaflet tends to be obtuse in the southern parts of the tree's range but acute in the north.

Flowers are on short stalks in large panicles above the foliage. The velvety brown buds open to small four-petalled, whitish individual flowers in November. The fleshy, two to three-lobed, rusty hairy, yellow fruits (capsules) contain orange-red acidic pulp which can be used for making jam or drinks.

Timber is close-grained and has been used for cabinet and structural work.

Although rarely seen in cultivation, this is an ornamental shade or specimen tree for deep, rich soils along the east coast of Australia where perhaps it could be grown more than it is.

Another species, *D. campbellii* E. Cheel, occurs in the Tweed River district. It differs in its smaller leaflets and absence of brown hairs on the young branchlets and leaf stalks.

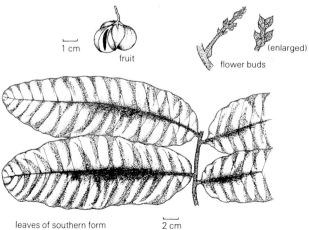

fruit

1 cm

flower buds

(enlarged)

leaves of southern form

2 cm

PITURI, CORKWOOD

Duboisia hopwoodii (F. Muell.) F. Muell.
SOLANACEAE

Pituri is a small but attractive tree, or large shrub, with bright green, shining willowy foliage which is poisonous to stock — it is one of the most virulent of Australia's poison plants. Its foliage was used by the Aboriginals to poison waterholes and stupefy emus, thus rendering them easy to kill. The Aboriginals also prized it as a drug, the leaves and twigs being ground and chewed or smoked.

The tree occurs in all mainland States except Victoria, favouring sandy soils in low rainfall areas. In Western Australia, where it is common in the pastoral country, the western boundary of its range virtually coincides with the eastern limit of the wheatlands. In South Australia it is only found in the far north-west. In New South Wales it is a frequent companion of the Bimble Box (*Eucalyptus populnea*) and can often be seen in woodland adjacent to the Barrier Highway, particularly in the Cobar district.

Conspicuous in this environment, the trees are neat and bushy with soft, satiny, smooth, linear leaves 4–12 cm long by usually 2–5 mm wide, but sometimes wider, with a strong odour. Bark is rough and grey, corky near the base.

The small, white, bell-shaped flowers with violet striations in the throat are produced in small axillary and terminal panicles in spring. These are followed by small black berries which are relished by birds.

Regeneration can occur from the rootstocks, this feature often resulting in the tree being seen in small, intimate clumps among its larger tree companions.

The genus, which has three species endemic to Australia, extends into New Caledonia. It provides alkaloids for the pharmaceutical industry.

The author has no knowledge of this species in cultivation.

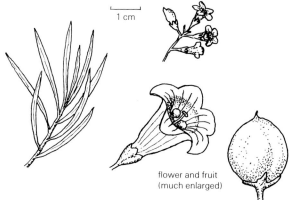

1 cm

flower and fruit
(much enlarged)

BLUE QUANDONG, BLUE FIG, BRACELET TREE

Elaeocarpus grandis F. Muell.
ELAEOCARPACEAE

Native to the coastal brush forests of northern New South Wales to northern Queensland, Blue Quandong is a member of a large, mainly tropical genus of plants from the Southern Hemisphere. There are about twenty Australian species, all endemic. Several of these are large trees native only to tropical Australia, but one species, *E. reticulatus*, extends south as far as Tasmania.

The genus is distinguished by the smooth lobeless fruits (drupes) with a fleshy outer covering enclosing a hard stone.

Blue Quandong is a large tree over 33 m in height, with a tall, strongly buttressed trunk supporting a slightly wrinkled, dark grey bark. The smooth leaves are thinly textured, with rather conspicuous veins and finely serrated margins, oblong-lanceolate in shape, 10–15 cm long by about 2·5 cm broad. As they age they change colour, until, just before they fall, they are an attractive bright red — at least in cooler, drier climates. The flowers, which resemble the Lily of the Valley, are large and fringed, greenish white in colour, and borne thickly in one-sided axillary racemes during spring. The bright blue quandong-shaped fruits that follow are very decorative and give rise to the tree's common name. They enclose a hard, deeply wrinkled, 5-celled stone, the mature cells each containing a solitary, narrowly oval seed. These stones are sometimes used to make necklaces.

The useful timber is pale yellow, soft and light.

BLUEBERRY ASH *E. reticulatus* Smith (syn. *E. cyaneus* Ait.). Sometimes called Lily of the Valley Tree, this species is a much smaller, dense, bushy tree, but just as ornamental with similar flowers and elliptical-shaped blue fruits. It is widespread from Fraser Island off the Queensland coast throughout the east coast regions to Tasmania.

E. obovatus G. Don, also known as Blueberry Ash, is a closely related larger tree that is found from near Sydney northwards to west of Bundaberg (Mount Perry) in Queensland.

Although rarely grown, these species are very decorative trees which are seldom too large for average gardens away from the tropics. They prefer moist, lime-free soils.

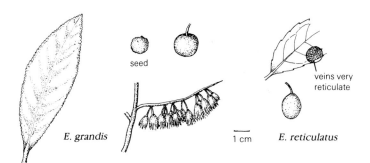

seed

E. grandis

veins very
reticulate

1 cm

E. reticulatus

LONG-LEAVED EMU BUSH, BERRIGAN

Eremophila longifolia (R. Br.) F. Muell.
MYOPORACEAE

Long-leaved Emu Bush is a small tree member of a genus comprising mainly bushy shrubs with rather showy tubular flowers and usually favouring poor limestone soils in low-rainfall areas of Australia. This particular species is found in all States in arid inland locations, often seen at its best along creek banks or sheltered gullies. It occurs mainly as single specimens, seldom more than two or three together.

The genus is purely Australian, consisting of about 180 species. The name was derived from the Greek *eremophiles*, meaning 'desert-loving'. The fruits are a favourite food of the emu, and young seedlings of the bushes are sometimes obtained from emu droppings.

Long-leaved Emu Bush is usually a tree to 7–8 m high with many graceful, drooping branches and a slender stem seldom reaching 30 cm in diameter. It often forms many root suckers. The rugged bark is brown and deeply fissured and resembles that of the Sugarwood, *Myoporum platycarpum* (see p. 266), a tree with which it is often associated.

As its name implies, the dark olive-green leaves are long and drooping, up to 20 cm long by 6 mm broad. They are very hairy when young, but at maturity are smooth, scattered, flat, and rather thick or fleshy. The tubular, often solitary flowers are pendulous, hairy, and deeply lobed at the mouth, usually a dull red or pink in colour, and spotted. They occur at various times throughout the year. The fruits are succulent egg-shaped drupes with a long slender style attached until maturity.

The timber is pale brown, hard, and close-grained.

This tree is a useful shelter and fodder tree in arid parts, particularly on calcareous soils, and could well be used for ornamental purposes in inland towns where the choice of a small shade tree is limited. It is protected by law in South Australia.

BUDDA *E. mitchellii* Benth. is a species from the western plains of New South Wales which sometimes forms a small graceful tree. The leaves are much shorter than those of *E. longifolia* (2–7 cm) and the flowers are fragrant and purple or white in colour. The timber of this tree is white-ant-resistant and useful for fence posts.

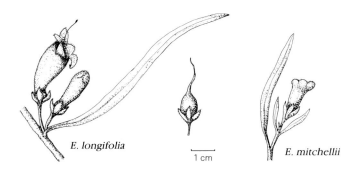

E. longifolia

1 cm

E. mitchellii

BATS-WING CORAL TREE, BEAN TREE

Erythrina vespertilio Benth.

FABACEAE

The coral trees belong to the tropical or subtropical parts of the world, several species being commonly cultivated in Australia. The Australian species *E. vespertilio* is no exception, and is mainly found growing in the monsoonal areas of north and north-east Australia. It extends to the rainforest of the east coast and to the dry Centre, and south to near Oodnadatta in South Australia, but is essentially a tree of the dry sclerophyll forests of the north. In common with several other trees of the monsoonal regions, it drops its leaves at the end of the 'dry' (early summer), flowers, and then produces new leaves.

In the east coast forests the tree is sometimes tall and upright to nearly 33 m in height, but elsewhere, and in cultivation, it is only small, seldom exceeding 10 m. It is variable in habit, foliage, and colour of flowers, but is often sparsely branched with little spread. Bark is slightly rough, and attractively marked with longitudinal lines or slits on its surface. The branches are covered with sharp, woody prickles that resemble rose thorns. The unusual leaves are pinnate, consisting of three leaflets, and are borne on long petioles. They occur in two distinct shapes, one resembling the extended wings of a bat, from which the common name is derived.

Flowers are large, curved, and pea-shaped, the colour varying from pink to a brilliant orange-red. These are prominently displayed in axillary racemes on stems devoid of leaves, and are very conspicuous, particularly in the open forests of their native habitat where they can be seen standing above the dry undergrowth. The oval-shaped, bean-like seeds are a glossy red or yellow, and are contained in pods 5–8 cm long. The Aboriginals used the seeds for making necklaces.

The timber is soft and spongy, and was used by Aboriginals for making shields.

This tree is occasionally cultivated, and grows quite well as far south as Adelaide, but has rarely been known to produce flowers in that city. A better-known species in cultivation is *E. variegata* L. from northern Queensland. The more commonly cultivated Coral Tree, frequently seen in Adelaide and Perth, is not of Australian origin.

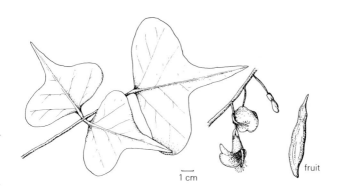

1 cm

fruit

POWDER-BARKED WANDOO

Eucalyptus accedens W. V. Fitzg.

MYRTACEAE

Powder-Barked Wandoo is a member of the well-known *Eucalyptus* genus, and is found only in Western Australia. It is a tree usually found on lateritic gravelly soils, particularly at elevations, and is not uncommon in the Darling Range, extending to the relatively dry sclerophyll woodlands of the inland slopes and nearby plains.

Eucalypts are the dominant tree species of the Australian continent, being found in every environment except the very arid deserts of the inland, and the pure tropical rainforests of parts of the east coast. Within these vastly differing environments many forms occur, from tall forest giants such as Mountain Ash to small, stunted, or shrubby mallees. Various names have been given to the different types, such as 'bloodwoods', 'stringybarks', 'boxes', 'peppermints', 'marlocks', and so on. There are more than 500 recorded species, although these hybridise quite freely within certain botanical groups, sometimes making positive identification difficult.

Eucalypts are valued throughout the world for ornament, hardwood timber, and conservation purposes, particularly in arid lands.

The genus is characterised by the flowers, which are without petals and are covered before opening by an operculum or cap. It is this feature which gives the genus its name, *eu* meaning 'well', and *kalyptos* meaning 'covered'. This operculum appears in many different shapes in the various species.

The operculum of the Powder-Barked Wandoo is a simple, smooth, domed shape. The tree itself is medium-sized, 15–25 m high, often with a well-branched crown, and with pale whitish to orange-coloured bark covered with a smooth talc-like powder. It flowers in early summer.

WANDOO *E. wandoo* Blakely (syn. *E. redunca* Schau. var. *elata* Benth.), a tree of similar areas of Western Australia, but usually on heavier clay soils, resembles *E. accedens* in appearance except that the bark is not powdery and is coloured white or mottled grey. Its botanical features are not similar. The hard timber is noted for its durability.

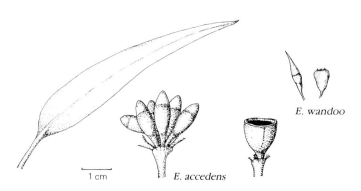

E. accedens

1 cm

E. wandoo

RIVER RED GUM

Eucalyptus camaldulensis Dehnh. var. *camaldulensis*
MYRTACEAE

River Red Gum is the most widespread, the best-known, and probably the best-loved of all the Australian eucalypt trees.

Artists and photographers have further enhanced its popularity by featuring it so often in their work that it has become almost a symbol of the Australian landscape.

The tree occurs in all States except Tasmania, usually following the banks of streams. Indeed, in dry open country a watercourse can easily be traced by simply following the line of River Red Gums.

It is a variable tree and appears in quite a number of different forms. Typically it is a large, gnarled, and wide-spreading tree of great character. The main trunk is thick, 1–2 m in diameter, with bark rough at the base but smooth and mottled above, usually grey and brown or cream in colour, often beautifully marked. Foliage varies from green to blue-green, the leaves often being long and narrow; some forms are distinctly weeping. Buds and fruits also vary throughout its range. Flowers are small and creamy white, and usually occur in summer months.

In northern and central Australia, the tree has a slender, smooth, white trunk and a more sparsely foliaged crown. It is this form, *E. camaldulensis* Dehnh. var. *obtusa* Blakely, which is often mistaken for Ghost Gum (*E. papuana*).

River Red Gum, despite its natural habit of following watercourses, is very easy to grow under other conditions. It is an ideal tree for farms, giving shade and shelter to stock, and feed can be grown right up to the trunk, but it has a bad habit of dropping limbs — particularly during hot weather — without warning and should not be planted too close to dwellings.

In northern Western Australia another tree, the FLOODED GUM *E. rudis* Endl., occurs in association with and could be easily mistaken for River Red Gum, although in the south it has a rough, fibrous bark, and is easily distinguished. This tree should not be confused with the eastern Flooded Gum (*E. grandis*), a giant, shaft-like tree of the Queensland and New South Wales forests (see p. 150).

var. *obtusa*

1 cm

LEMON-SCENTED GUM

Eucalyptus citriodora Hook.
MYRTACEAE

Well known in cultivation owing to its adaptability and its ornamental appearance, Lemon-scented Gum has a naturally confined habitat range in Queensland. Occurring between Mackay
and Maryborough along the coast, it extends some 300 km
inland, and is also found in a limited area of the Atherton
Tableland.

A feature of a number of eucalypts is their bark. Many of the
smooth-barked species, particularly just after deciduating
usually in late summer, assume mottled colourations which are
often very beautiful. Others have smooth, polished, brown
bark, like the Gimlet Gum (*E. salubris*), or rough, furrowed
bark like the 'ironbark' group, but the bark is always an
attractive feature of the tree.

Lemon-scented Gum is no exception, being a particularly
graceful tree with a long, shaft-like trunk, the bark a smooth
greyish white or a lovely pinkish colour in some specimens. It
is one of the 'bloodwoods', and a valuable timber tree, reaching
45 m high under favourable conditions. The crown is usually
symmetrical with sparse, but graceful and rather drooping,
foliage.

Juvenile leaves are rough and hairy, but become long and
smooth, narrow to broadly lanceolate, at maturity. The oil in
the leaves is rich in citronella, which has a commercial use as
well as giving the foliage a pleasant lemon aroma, especially
when crushed.

Flowers are white, and although not spectacular, appear in
quite large, attractive clusters, usually in October–November.

SPOTTED GUM *E. maculata* Hook. is a near relation which
is often visually difficult to distinguish from Lemon-scented
Gum. Usually it is more densely branched and has a mottled or
spotted grey bark, but the true test is the leaves, which have no
lemon scent when crushed. This species is widespread from
Queensland to eastern Victoria, where the Spotted Gum forests
are a feature of parts of the landscape.

Both species are easily grown provided frosts are not severe
and rainfall exceeds about 400 mm. They are both rapid
growers. Lemon-scented Gum has very brittle branches which
may snap off without warning, particularly in windy weather.

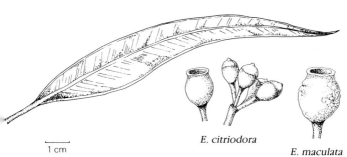

E. citriodora

E. maculata

1 cm

SUGAR GUM

Eucalyptus cladocalyx F. Muell.
MYRTACEAE

Sugar Gum was once planted more often on farms as a shelterbelt tree than any other eucalypt, at least in the wheat districts of Victoria, South Australia, and Western Australia.

Its natural habitat is quite restricted, the tree being native only to South Australia in the southern Flinders Ranges, on Kangaroo Island, and, as a dwarfed form, on Eyre Peninsula. Climate is temperate with hot dry summers and cool to mild winters. Rainfall is 350–600 mm, most of it falling in winter.

At its best, Sugar Gum grows to a height of 35 m with a trunk 1–2 m in diameter. Its habit is to produce several long, steeply angled main branches from about halfway up the trunk, each branch being clothed in a small rounded canopy of shiny foliage. The bark is shed in irregular patches, leaving a smooth, mottled effect in colours of orange, brown, grey, and white. The leaves are narrow to broad, lanceolate and glossy. The flowers, which occur in axillary and terminal umbels, are creamy yellow in colour, and quite prominently displayed in summer.

Sugar Gum recovers from hard cutting very well, and this fact has led to its being periodically pollarded or lopped to produce bushy new growth for windbreak purposes. Unfortunately pollarding these trees has become such a habit that they are treated in this way in many situations where it is quite unnecessary, and the beauty of a well-developed unpruned tree is seldom seen.

Although the Sugar Gum is easily grown in the climate and soils suited to wheat growing, many other species form naturally better windbreaks and shelter trees in these areas. BUSHY SUGAR GUM *E. cladocalyx* 'Nana', a dwarf form of the same species which naturally grows to 10 m with a bushy, spreading crown, is one such tree. It is found only on lower Eyre Peninsula, South Australia.

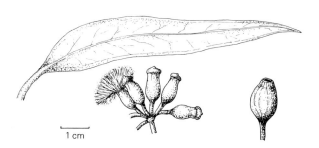

1 cm

KARRI

Eucalyptus diversicolor F. Muell.
MYRTACEAE

Karri is a tall and majestic forest tree up to 85 m in height. It is the tallest tree found in Western Australia, where it can be seen dominating the vegetation wherever it grows. The habitat range of Karri is restricted to a relatively small area of the south-west, from near Albany to Cape Leeuwin, on deep loamy soils where rainfall is in excess of 1000 mm annually. Here, the Karri forests are a well-known tourist attraction.

The tree is a true 'gum' with smooth bark on a long shaft-like trunk. At the time the old bark is shed, the bark can be seen in varying colours of orange, yellow, grey and white. This feature gives to the tree its specific name of *diversicolor*. The leaves are broadly lanceolate, dark green above but paler underneath. The umbels of 3–6 white flowers produce a very high-grade honey which is generally recognised as the best in Western Australia.

The timber of the Karri and of Jarrah, which it closely resembles, are among Australia's most valued hardwoods. They are deep red in colour, hard, durable, easily worked and, in the case of Jarrah, resistant to termites and fungi. For this reason they are in much demand for commercial uses such as the construction of flooring boards and joists, railway sleepers, fence posts, wharves, and jetties. The bushman's test to distinguish the timber of these two trees is to burn a splinter; if it leaves a white ash it is Karri; if the ash is black or grey it is Jarrah.

JARRAH *E. marginata* Donn ex Smith is common in south-west Western Australia where rainfall is in excess of 750 mm. Usually a large forest tree, it is found in the sandy soils of the coastline, extending from Gin Gin, north of Perth (parts of Perth were originally Jarrah forest) to as far south as Albany. It is also very prevalent in the laterite or ironstone soils of the Darling Range and elsewhere.

The tree is a 'stringybark'. It attains a height of 40 m or more at its best, but also occurs in a stunted form only about 2 m high on the stony slopes of the Stirling Range and on rocky outcrops near Albany. Bark is dull grey, strong and fibrous and longitudinally fissured. Leaves are narrow, 5–8 cm long, and dull, dark green, paler underneath. The flowers, which occur in umbels of 4–8 during spring and summer, are white and particularly showy when seen on younger trees nearer eye level.

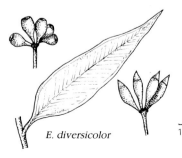

E. diversicolor

1 cm

E. marginata

SAND MALLEE

Eucalyptus eremophila Maiden
MYRTACEAE

A species native only to Western Australia, Sand Mallee enjoys an extensive range in the 200–450 mm rainfall zone. It is found in an area bounded approximately by Lake Moore in the north to Gnowangerup in the south, with an eastern limit as far as Balladonia.

Throughout this range the species varies quite appreciably, especially in the flowers and fruits. It is closely related to Flat-topped Yate (*E. occidentalis*), and, in fact, was once described as a variety under that name.

A good deal of its habitat has now been cleared but it can still be found in places forming open thickets, or on the sides of roads, usually in sand, or red alkaline loam.

Sand Mallee is a single- or multi-stemmed tree, 5–8 m in height, with smooth, polished brown bark which is shed in late summer. Leaves are narrow with a flattened stalk, grey-green to blue-green in colour.

Flowering occurs from June to November. The flowers are prolific and beautiful and make this tree one of the most orna-mental of the flowering mallees, particularly when a good form is chosen. They vary from pale greenish yellow to deep glow-ing yellow, or, rarely, a dull red colour. These large flowers droop downwards in clusters of 3–7 arranged on a long, flat-tened stalk. The operculum is variable, but typically long and curved and narrower at the base than the hypanthium or flower cup. The buds are a polished reddish brown before the flowers open.

With the ever-increasing interest in growing native trees in Australia, where a small but ornamental eucalypt is required, Sand Mallee could well receive favourable consideration. It is particularly suited to a climate such as that of Adelaide or many of the country towns in Australia with a low to moderate rain-fall and often alkaline soils. It is also an excellent windbreak species for planting on farms in dry sandy soil areas.

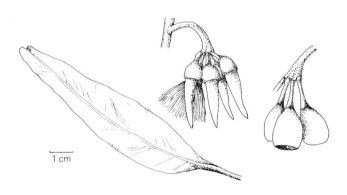

1 cm

ILLYARRIE, RED CAP GUM

Eucalyptus erythrocorys F. Muell.

MYRTACEAE

Only a small tree 3–10 m high, Illyarrie possesses flowers which, even among the eucalypts, are unique and very beautiful. It is this feature which has earned it popularity as a cultivated specimen tree.

Naturally inhabiting quite a restricted area in the Irwin River – Shark Bay coastal districts of Western Australia, it is almost always found on limestone soils with a rainfall of about 350 mm or less.

The juvenile leaves of seedlings or new shoots are rough and furry. Seedlings at this stage of growth are slow and difficult to establish, particularly in areas of extreme cold. Young trees should be grown in containers for 2 years, then planted out. At this stage they mature rapidly to a small, bushy tree with long, rather thick and narrow, usually opposite, curved leaves that are a rich glossy green. As the tree develops it grows more slender with sparse, drooping branches, and flowers mainly at the top of the plant. In time, if flowers are a major consideration, it sometimes pays to pollard the tree at ground level, a treatment from which it recovers rapidly.

Bark is smooth and white just after deciduating, but turns pale grey as it ages, with occasional persistent patches of a roughish texture.

The flowers, either single or in umbels of two or three, consist of a bright red biretta-like cap which falls to reveal stamens at first greenish yellow, later turning to bright sulphur yellow. These are grouped together in four tufts, each individual flower 5 cm or more across. Flowering is often prolific and spectacular, particularly on young trees, with the red opercula and yellow stamens visible at the one time from March to June. Fruits are large and woody, bell-shaped with rather prominent ribbing, the summit a smooth reddish disc for a year or so. The timber is quite soft and brittle for a eucalypt, and is easily cut.

Illyarrie succeeds on practically any soil in a warm, dry climate. It is now well established as a cultivated specimen, particularly in South and Western Australia where the climate is suitable.

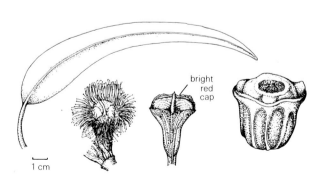

bright
red
cap

1 cm

LINDSAY GUM, WHITE MALLEE

Eucalyptus erythronema Turcz. var. *erythronema*
MYRTACEAE

Lindsay Gum has a fairly extensive but scattered range through-out areas of farmland in the drier parts of Western Australia receiving a 300–500 mm rainfall. It is never found in large stands, but is prone to occur in small isolated groups, usually among other species, such as Gimlet Gum. It favours heavy clay soils which usually indicate land excellent for agriculture.

Although sometimes cultivated, Lindsay Gum then seldom, if ever, attains the beauty of form which characterises the tree under natural conditions. It is usually found in mallee form, 5–8 m high, with a broad rootstock supporting several slender main stems. These often assume irregular and somewhat con-torted outlines which display the tree to its best advantage. The bark is a gleaming white (sometimes pinkish), being covered with a smooth, white, talc-like powder which persists to the smaller branches. When the outer bark decorticates it reveals a pale green smooth surface beneath, which combines with patches of old bark to create a striking effect.

Branches are erect, fairly sparsely foliaged with deep, lustrous green, rather narrow, but thick, leaves. These are rich in oil and could have some commercial value. The flowers are borne in showy pendulous clusters on long stalks (pedicels). Usually a brilliant red, they are sometimes a creamy yellow colour; they are rich in nectar, and very attractive to bees. Flowering occurs from August to January. Fruits are bell-shaped and about 12 mm in length.

A smaller-growing form of this tree occurs north of Perth scattered throughout various districts usually on stony soils. It has been recorded as *E. erythronema* var. *marginata* Benth.

The Lindsay Gum is a particularly ornamental flowering euca-lypt, well worthy of garden culture in most soils in areas of low to moderate rainfall.

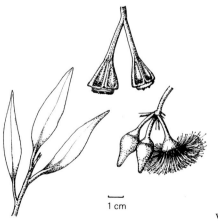

1 cm

var. *marginata*

WESTERN AUSTRALIAN RED FLOWERING GUM

Eucalyptus ficifolia F. Muell.

MYRTACEAE

This tree, which closely resembles the Marri (*E. calophylla*) but is usually much smaller, is well known throughout the world as an ornamental flowering specimen tree, although many of the garden-grown flowering gums of today are hybrids between the two species. Flowers of the true *E. ficifolia* are usually a vivid vermilion, although flower colours now vary considerably in the pink to red range. The flowers usually occur from November to February, but may be later in cooler districts.

Its natural occurrence, near Albany in Western Australia, is very restricted, and the tree is seldom seen under natural conditions.

Western Australian Red Flowering Gum is a true 'blood-wood', possessing friable bark, a characteristic leaf with parallel lateral nerves which spread from the midrib almost at right angles, and umbels of flowers arranged in large panicles. The operculum (bud cap) has a tendency to hang on after the flower opens. Urn-shaped fruits are large and woody.

The tree is variable, but rarely more than 8 m high, with a dense crown of heavy foliage. It is extensively cultivated, favouring moist, sandy soils but adapting well to heavier soils, and preferring a temperate climate.

MARRI *E. calophylla* R. Br. is one of the largest and commonest trees of the Jarrah and Karri forests of south-west Western Australia. In the northern and eastern limits of its range, however, it is considerably reduced in stature.

Sometimes known as Port Gregory Gum, it extends along the coastal regions from Port Gregory near the Murchison River in the north to Cape Riche in the south, and inland to slightly beyond the Jarrah country. Within this range it favours light sandy soils, particularly near the coast.

The tree is a handsome ornamental specimen, reaching over 35 m high under favourable conditions, with a dense, spreading crown which gives ample shade. The large pink or, more often, white flowers are prominently displayed above the foliage, and occur in masses which make a fine sight in summer.

It is an excellent tree for apiarists.

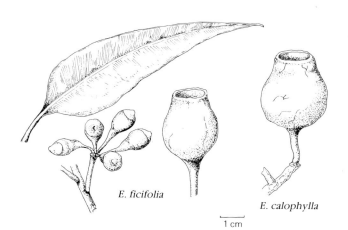

E. ficifolia

E. calophylla

|—— 1 cm

TASMANIAN BLUE GUM

Eucalyptus globulus Labill. subsp. *globulus*
MYRTACEAE

This tree is sometimes known as Southern Blue Gum, but the common name Tasmanian Blue Gum would seem more apt when one considers that the flowers of this tree have been adopted as Tasmania's floral emblem.

It is a large forest tree, 50–70 m high under favourable conditions, inhabiting the south-east coast of Tasmania and restricted areas of Victoria at Wilson's Promontory and the Otway Ranges. Climate is cool to mild, with wet winters, annual rainfall up to 1400 mm. Tasmanian Blue Gum usually inhabits hilly country or moist valleys in deep, rich soils.

The tree is tall and straight-trunked, 1–2 m in diameter, with smooth bark except at the base. The bark is coloured in patches of grey or grey-blue and sheds in long strips. Juvenile leaves and stems are mealy blue and persist for some time. The leaves are broad, opposite and stem-clasping, the stems square. Mature leaves, however, are alternate, long and narrow, curved, and a dark glossy green.

The flowers, which occur from June to November, are quite large and a deep attractive cream. Timber is light yellowish brown, strong, and durable.

This tree is commonly cultivated as Blue Gum, but is not really suitable for suburban gardens because of the size to which it eventually grows. It is, however, very adaptable as far as soil requirements go, grows extremely rapidly, is quite happy in hot dry climates such as Adelaide's, and can be recommended for parks and large gardens. Attacked by borers.

Tasmanian Blue Gum has been extensively planted overseas as a timber tree, and is well known for its extremely rapid growth, particularly in South Africa.

SOUTHERN BLUE GUM or EURABBIE *E. globulus* Labill. subsp. *bicostata* (Maiden et al.) Kirkpatr. is a closely allied species from the high-rainfall eucalypt forests of Victoria and New South Wales, and MAIDEN'S GUM *E. globulus* Labill. subsp. *maidenii* (F. Muell.) Kirkpatr. is another related Blue Gum of the high country of those two States.

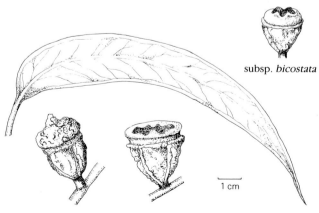

subsp. *bicostata*

1 cm

ROSE GUM, FLOODED GUM

Eucalyptus grandis Hill ex Maiden
MYRTACEAE

One of Australia's finest forest eucalypts is undoubtedly the
Rose Gum, a tall, straight, white-trunked tree of the high-rainfall
(1000–1800 mm) coastal belt of New South Wales and Queensland. Its main range is from just north of Sydney to south-
eastern Queensland, but isolated occurrences are also found
near Mackay and on the Atherton Tableland in north Queensland.

It is mainly found in the mountain ranges and fertile valleys
where soils are deep rich loams, often of basalt origin. These
soils support subtropical rainforest with which Rose Gum
merges; here it can be seen rising majestically above young
rainforest vegetation in the manner portrayed in the picture on
the opposite page.

Rose Gum grows to a height of about 50–60 m at its best,
with a smooth, straight, powdery white bole up to 2 m in diameter. At the base it is covered with a short stocking of persistent,
rough and fibrous grey bark. The main trunk often extends
30 m or more up to the first branches. Leaves are a glossy green
with a paler undersurface, lanceolate, slightly wavy and tapering to a long point. The white flowers appear in winter in axillary umbels on flattened stalks, 7–12 flowers per umbel, and the
fruits are pear-shaped with protruding valves.

It is a commonly milled tree, being noted for its rose-red
timber, which is softer and lighter than most eucalypt
hardwoods. The timber is easily worked and suited to many
commercial uses.

Rose Gum is a very rapid-growing tree which is adaptable to
soil and climate where rainfall is adequate. It grows well as far
south as Adelaide in the higher-rainfall hills and foothills regions
where it is sometimes cultivated. Plantations on farmland in
northern New South Wales where fertilisers are used have
produced 7 m of growth in the first year after planting.

SYDNEY BLUE GUM *E. saligna* Smith is another majestic
forest tree of similar character. It is found in parts of the
southern habitat range of Rose Gum, with which it is easily
confused. Its fruits are also very similar to those of Rose Gum
but are cylindrical or slightly bell-shaped with protruding
valves, whilst the leaves are narrower. In contrast to Rose Gum,
Sydney Blue Gum is seldom found in pure stands and its timber
is harder and stronger.

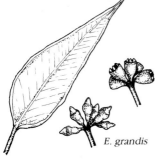

E. grandis

E. saligna

1 cm

BLACK BOX, RIVER BOX

Eucalyptus largiflorens F. Muell.

MYRTACEAE

Black Box is a medium- to occasionally large-sized tree which is extremely widespread throughout the dry plains of western New South Wales, and extends into Queensland, Victoria, and South Australia. In these parts of New South Wales it is one of the principal eucalypts, often occurring in pure stands, but it is also found associated with other trees such as Drooping Myall (*Acacia pendula*) and the Native Willow (*Acacia salicina*).

Although climate is dry, with summer shade temperatures exceeding 38°C, rainfall 250–400 mm and droughts not uncommon, the tree occurs on low-lying depressions and river flats which are subjected to periodic flooding. Soils are usually clays or clay loams with poor drainage.

It is a very common tree in the Upper Murray districts of South Australia, where it sometimes appears in an almost willow-like form, with drooping grey-blue foliage contrasting strikingly with the tree's rough black bark. In such areas as these where stands of Black Box still dominate their environment, one is able to realise the great beauty of this often neglected Australian tree.

Black Box is a low-branched tree, 10–25 m high, with a trunk up to 1 m in diameter and an open but wide-spreading crown that can provide good shade for stock. The rough bark is persistent, often to the smaller branches, dark grey to black, and deeply furrowed. Leaves are a dull grey-blue in colour, rather narrow and pointed, up to 12 cm long.

Flowers are small and creamy or white but prolific, and occur in terminal or axillary panicles in spring and summer.

Timber is pink or reddish brown, heavy and hard, and an excellent fuel.

Despite its dry habitat, Black Box only frequents areas where underground water is present and is a particularly good species for planting on soils which become flooded and waterlogged after heavy rains. It also tolerates salt and limestone and is a useful species where these hard conditions prevail.

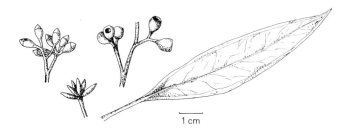

1 cm

YELLOW GUM, SOUTH AUSTRALIAN BLUE GUM

Eucalyptus leucoxylon F. Muell. subsp. *leucoxylon*
MYRTACEAE

Yellow Gum, or Blue Gum, as it is known in South Australia, is a fairly common tree of the higher-rainfall zones of South Australia, and of western Victoria.

In South Australia it is well known in the Mount Lofty Ranges, from which it extends as far north as the lower Flinders Range. It also occurs in the south-east as well as to a minor degree on Kangaroo Island and Eyre Peninsula (as *E. leucoxylon* F. Muell. subsp. *petiolaris* Boland, a smaller tree).

Climate is temperate, with cool, often frosty winters, but summer heat exceeding 38°C on occasions. Rainfall is 500–1000 mm.

Yellow Gum can be a medium to tall and spreading tree, or reasonably slender, 14–28 m in height. Bark is smooth, white or creamish mottled grey, rough and persistent at the base. Leaves are broad, dull green, and in opposite pairs in the juvenile stage, but up to 15 cm long, alternate, and with a prominent central vein at maturity. Flowers are quite large, usually in threes, and white, cream, or various shades of attractive pink to red. On Eyre Peninsula the subspecies *petiolaris* sometimes has bright yellow flowers. Flowering occurs in autumn and winter. Timber is pale, tough, strong, and durable.

Yellow Gum is a large, ornamental tree preferring heavy-textured clay soils in its natural habitat, but tolerant of a range of soils, including limestone, when cultivated. It is a relatively easy species to grow, much loved by birds and an excellent honey tree.

A smaller-growing form with larger fruits, *E. leucoxylon* F. Muell. subsp. *megalocarpa* Boland, is mainly found in South Australia's south-east coastal areas. It is a much bushier, lower-growing tree, with broad leaves. The flowers are usually large and often a striking deep pink in colour, occurring from April to June.

SCRUBBY BLUE GUM *E. leucoxylon* F. Muell. subsp. *pruinosa* (F. Muell. ex Miq.) Boland is a poorer-growing form from north central Victoria and inland South Australia, usually in about the 400–500 mm rainfall range.

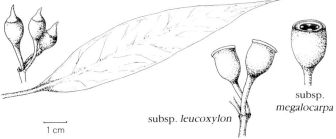

subsp. *leucoxylon*

subsp. *megalocarpa*

1 cm

LONG-FLOWERED MARLOCK

Eucalyptus macrandra F. Muell. ex Benth.

MYRTACEAE

Although this tree is usually a scrubby mallee growing in thickets in the wild, it has become increasingly popular for garden culture because of its showy, often spectacular flowers, small stature, and ability to succeed near the sea, even growing in reasonably saline soils.

It is native only to a fairly restricted area of Western Australia, mainly growing along stream banks and in moist depressions, from the Stirling and Porongorup Ranges eastwards to the Phillips River. Climate here is temperate, with cold winters and hot summers, annual rainfall ranging from approximately 400 mm to 750 mm.

In mallee form the tree rarely exceeds 3 m, but occasionally it grows as a single-stemmed tree to about 7 m high. The bark is smooth and shining, light brown when fresh but turns grey before deciduating. Leaves are lanceolate and thick, with a dull, metallic sheen that gives them a quite attractive bluish look.

The distinguishing features of this tree are its long, narrow, horn-like opercula or bud caps, its densely clustered umbels of flower buds (up to fifteen per umbel), and then the opened bright yellow fluffy flowers. These normally appear from January to March. They are succeeded by clusters of cup-shaped, woody fruits on slightly flattened peduncles.

In cultivation Long-flowered Marlock remains a small bushy tree and is suited to most conditions in areas of temperate climate and moderate rainfall. It is particularly useful for coastal planting, where it has proved to be one of the very best eucalypts to withstand wind and soils rearward of foreshore plantations. Many specimens can be seen in the West Lakes development in Adelaide.

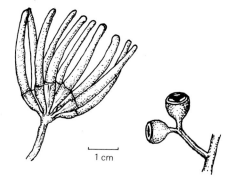

1 cm

YELLOW BOX

Eucalyptus melliodora Cunn. ex Schauer
MYRTACEAE

Yellow Box is a common tree of the inland slopes of the Great Dividing Range in Victoria and New South Wales. It is also found to a minor degree on the tablelands of New South Wales and in isolated areas of south-eastern Queensland.

Its typical habitat, however, is found on the gentle slopes of open woodland, occurring in the 350–850 mm rainfall zone in a temperate climate with cool wet winters and hot dry summers.

Associated trees in this terrain are other 'box' eucalypts such as Red Box (*E. polyanthemos*) and some of the 'ironbark' group, which are closely related. Hybrids between the two groups are not uncommon.

In its lower rainfall range Yellow Box is usually found in flats and depressions which collect some water during wet periods.

It is quite a large tree, 20–35 m high, with a rounded, spreading crown, and a trunk 60–90 cm in diameter which extends about one-third of the total height before the first branches appear. The brown bark is rough, persistent, and friable over the trunk and lower branches but becomes smooth and pale-coloured on the smaller branches. The foliage is usually grey-blue, thus contrasting well with the brownish trunk and larger branches to give the tree a handsome overall appearance. Yellow Box is, however, quite variable in form and is not always seen as described above.

The flowers appear in umbels of 3–7 at the ends of the twigs, a feature of 'box' and 'ironbark' eucalypts. They are cream in colour — although there is a rare pink-flowering form — and are prolific, making this one of the best honey trees of the genus. Flowering occurs from October to February.

Timber is pale yellow, hard, strong, and durable, with a close grain. It is prized as fuel.

Yellow Box is a tree which is adaptable to cultivation, preferring good loamy soils, and should be more extensively cultivated as a large tree in parks and gardens in temperate climates with a rainfall exceeding 350 mm.

1 cm

TALLOW WOOD

Eucalyptus microcorys F. Muell.
MYRTACEAE

Tallow Wood is a large forest tree, probably the most common in northern coastal New South Wales and southern Queensland. It is usually found in hilly or mountainous country where humidity is high, and rainfall 900–1500 mm annually (most of it falling in summer).

This eucalypt is unusual in that it is sometimes found as an overstorey species in true rainforest. Favouring a warm temperate to subtropical climate, it also occurs in the tablelands of New South Wales in areas of frosts and snow. Frequent companions of Tallow Wood are Sydney Blue Gum (*E. saligna*) and Blackbutt (*E. pilularis*).

A mature tree reaches 30–50 m. It has a long straight trunk and compact crown; the first branches appear at a point about two-thirds the total height. A lovely feature of the tree is the light brown persistent bark, which is soft and spongy, fibrous, and deeply furrowed, with corky patches. Leaves are bright, shiny green, rather broadly lanceolate, and sharply pointed. The flowers, small and white, appear in axillary or terminal panicles from July to November. The bark colour and leaves make it an easily distinguished tree amongst its forest companions.

Tallow Wood timber is well known and prized as a handsome flooring. It is yellowish or light brown, strong, hard, and durable. The greasy surface makes it easy to work and polish and it has many commercial uses.

This tree grows quite well on good soils in the cool Mount Lofty Ranges near Adelaide, which is well outside its natural occurrence. It forms a handsome specimen tree, at least while relatively young, often growing more spreading, sometimes multistemmed, with a dense, rich green canopy of foliage.

BASTARD TALLOW WOOD *E. planchoniana* F. Muell. is
a similar tree from much the same areas, but with thick, rather broad leaves, and much larger, entirely different flowers and fruits.

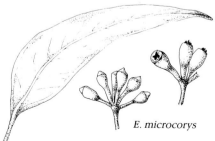

E. microcorys

1 cm

E. planchoniana

COOLABAH, COOLIBAH

Eucalyptus microtheca F. Muell.
MYRTACEAE

Coolabah is an inland tree of legendary fame.

It is found in the very low rainfall inland areas, occurring in all States except Victoria and Tasmania, but always inhabiting watercourses and depressions, usually with a clay subsoil. Coolabah is also found in the tropical north of Australia where climate is monsoonal.

In central Australia the typical Coolabah is a spreading tree with a thick, rough-barked trunk to 120 cm in diameter; smooth bark occurs only on the smaller branchlets. Its spread is often as great as its height — 14–20 m. It is a tree that provides ample shade where it is really needed.

In Western Australia it is common in the Kimberley division and here it occurs in much the same form as that just described. It extends south as far as the Murchison River area, and it is in this southern extremity of its range that it appears with a smooth, powdery white bark covering the trunk and branches, and could justifiably be judged a different species by the observer. This tree was known by the Aboriginals as *yathoo* or *callaille*.

Coolabah timber is the hardest of all eucalypt timbers, extremely strong, and termite-resistant. It is typically a dark brown colour but is traversed by whitish threads in the dense, interlocked grain.

The leaves are dull and leathery, lanceolate to oblong. As with most tropical trees, the small cup-shaped fruits are shed each year after flowering, making seed difficult to collect. The creamy yellow flowers are produced in summer.

GREY BOX *E. tectifica* F. Muell. is another Western Australian tree of the Kimberleys. It is very similar in its general appearance to the rough-barked Coolabah. This tree, however, is seldom seen near watercourses and depressions, as it inhabits the stony rises and hills of the same regions. Its fragile fruits are much larger, but deciduate each year also, and are therefore not always available for identification.

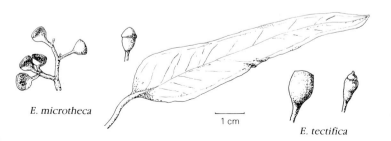

E. microtheca

1 cm

E. tectifica

WOOLLYBUTT, MELALEUCA GUM

Eucalyptus miniata Cunn. ex Schauer
MYRTACEAE

One of the larger eucalypts of northern tropical Australia, Woollybutt is found in a monsoonal climate with a 750–1500 mm rainfall, practically all of which occurs from December to April.

It extends from the northern Kimberleys in Western Australia, through the Northern Territory and into northern Queensland, usually favouring sandstone or quartzite soils, often in association with Darwin Stringybark (*E. tetrodonta* F. Muell.).

The name Woollybutt has originated from the persistent bark on the lower portions of the tree. This bark on it and on another northern species, *E. phoenicea* F. Muell., is quite different from that of any other of the *Eucalyptus* genus. It consists of numerous thin papery flakes, which, after decay has taken place, remain on the lower parts of the trunk, like pale brown netting.

The tree itself attains a height of 14–30 m but often less, with wide-spreading branches, the first branches occurring at about 7 m. The upper portion of the trunk and the branches is smooth and whitish; the small branchlets are powdery white. These contrast vividly with the broad green leaves and spectacular flowers.

The flowers are a feature of the tree. These are an intense orange-vermilion (hence the name *miniata*, meaning flame scarlet), quite large individually, and occurring in umbels of 3–7. The flower calyx is also a powdery white.

The tree blooms freely when quite young and small, displaying flowers where they can be easily admired. It flowers in June–July.

Timber is red and hard, but not of high quality, although it is used for milling purposes in the Darwin area.

This tree rivals Western Australian Red Flowering Gum (*E. ficifolia*) for floral beauty, and should certainly be used as an ornamental flowering tree where climate is suitable.

Little is known of its adaptability to cultivation in more temperate climates.

GNAINGAR *E. phoenicea* F. Muell. is a smaller tree up to 10 m high which is also noted for its lovely red flowers, up to 16 in each umbel. These are on slender pedicels, thus differing from those of the Woollybutt, which are without stalks.

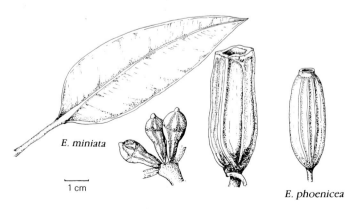

E. miniata

1 cm

E. phoenicea

MESSMATE STRINGYBARK, MESSMATE

Eucalyptus obliqua L'Her.
MYRTACEAE

Messmate Stringybark is a tall forest tree of mountainous and high-rainfall country in the cooler temperate regions of Australia, especially Victoria and Tasmania. It is also found in South Australia, particularly in the Mount Lofty Ranges where it is one of the dominant natural trees, in New South Wales, and to a lesser extent in southern Queensland.

It occurs in 750–1250 mm rainfall areas where climate is dry and mild in summer, but cold, wet, and often frosty in winter and early spring. The tree is often found in pure stands and where these are allowed to remain on cleared land, they add an attractive feature to the landscape. Parts of the Mount Lofty Ranges near Adelaide depend almost entirely on stands of Messmate Stringybark for their character and natural beauty.

The tree itself is usually straight and tall, 35–70 m high, with a trunk approximately two-thirds the total height, and 1–3 m (in large trees) in diameter. Bark is persistent, rough and fibrous, brown, but grey-coloured when old.

Leaves are long and broadly lanceolate, thick, and dark green on both sides. The new leaves and tips are a lovely bronze colour, often adding an attraction to young trees which is quite delightful, particularly when enhanced by the early morning or late evening sun.

The tree flowers abundantly in summer, the flowers being small and cream-coloured.

Messmate Stringybark timber is one of Australia's most important commercial timbers; it is particularly vital to the economy of Victoria and Tasmania. It is known as Australian or Tasmanian Oak and is used extensively for oak flooring as well as other structural work and furniture, and for pulp manufacture. The timber is brown or creamy brown in colour, hard, straight-grained, and easily worked.

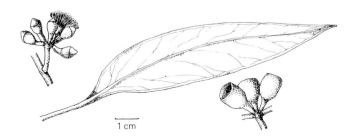

1 cm

GIANT MALLEE,
RED MALLEE, OIL MALLEE

Eucalyptus oleosa F. Muell. ex Miq.
MYRTACEAE

Eucalyptus oleosa is widespread throughout the drier regions of southern temperate Australia, extending from New South Wales in the east to Western Australia in the west. In common with many trees not restricted to a localised habitat, it occurs in many forms which are quite variable in appearance.

Some forms of *E. oleosa* have hybridised with associated species such as *E. foecunda* Schauer, and sometimes a positive identification is difficult, even for the trained botanist. Closely related trees include the smooth-barked Merrit (*E. flocktoniae* Maiden), Red Mallee (*E. socialis* F. Muell. ex Miq., p. 186) and Redwood (*E. transcontinentalis* Maiden, p. 186), and the rough, scaly-barked Yorrel or Red Morrel (*E. longicornis* F. Muell.).

E. oleosa occurs as a small, many-stemmed mallee, as a large tree of mallee habit, and occasionally as a slender single-stemmed tree.

Bark is usually grey and smooth, but rough at the base of the tree, or quite rough on the trunk and main branches. Leaves, too, are variable, often blue-green (glaucous) but sometimes bright green and shining. Flowers, which vary from pale cream to a very lovely pale lemon yellow, as in *E. socialis*, are usually abundant and attractive. Flowering time is variable, usually from May to December.

It is the fruits which retain their distinctive characteristics throughout the species. These are typically smooth and globular with a narrow rim, and deeply included valves with protruding needle-like points.

The specific name (*oleosa*) originated from the large oil content of the leaves, this tree being particularly useful for the production of eucalyptus oil.

Although Giant Mallee is seldom cultivated, good forms of this tree can be quite ornamental, and are particularly useful in dry alkaline soils in conditions where many trees are difficult to grow. It is a good honey tree.

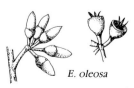

E. oleosa

1 cm

E. flocktoniae

E. longicornis

GHOST GUM

Eucalyptus papuana F. Muell.
MYRTACEAE

The Ghost Gum, a tree made famous by Aboriginal painters, has an extensive range over northern Australia, particularly the Northern Territory, as well as inhabiting savanna woodland near Port Moresby in Papua New Guinea.

Although principally a tree of the tropics, where climate is monsoonal, it is in the dry southern parts of its range in the Northern Territory and, to a lesser extent, Queensland, that this tree has earned its fame. Here it is often the only notable tree occurring over wide areas. It is in this part of its habitat that it contrasts vividly with the colourful landscape, and has become a feature of the artist's brush.

Under these drier more temperate conditions the Ghost Gum is usually found inhabiting river flats subjected to periodic flooding. These situations are where the River Red Gum, *E. camaldulensis* var. *obtusa*, also flourishes, and the latter is often mistaken for Ghost Gum in these areas, where it has very similar superficial characteristics.

Mature trees vary considerably within the habitat range, from a slender 7 m up to 25 m, and are well branched and spreading. In the drier zones the trunk is often slender and reaches 5 m or more before the first limbs. The bark is lustrous, smooth, and white, and contrasts with the leaves, which are deep green and shining.

The overall beauty of the tree is enhanced still further by the pendulous habit of the branchlets.

The small white flowers and urn-shaped fruits do not remain for long on the tree and for this reason seed of this species is not readily obtained. It normally flowers in summer.

Timber is pale red, dense, and hard.

Although it favours a tropical climate, the Ghost Gum has such an extensive range, embracing a number of different conditions, that it could possibly respond very well to cultivation in other areas.

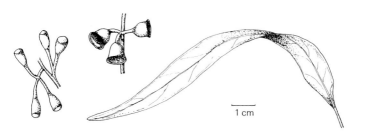

1 cm

SNOW GUM

Eucalyptus pauciflora Sieber ex Sprengel
subsp. *niphophila* (Maiden & Blakely) L. Johnson & Blaxell
MYRTACEAE

As its common name implies, Snow Gum is native only to the high altitudes (1300–2300 m) of Victoria and New South Wales where snow persists throughout the winter and early spring months.

It forms the limit of tree vegetation in these alpine areas and under the hardest climatic conditions of the region takes on its most attractive, if contorted, form. At lower altitudes and under less harsh conditions, however, it grows erect but loses its characteristic aged appearance. Here, other related trees, White Sally (*E. pauciflora* subsp. *pauciflora*) and Black Sally (*E. stellulata*) are also encountered, but these are never found above the 1800 m mark.

The tree itself is usually mallee-like, 5–8 m high, with a broad crown of foliage and a crooked, smooth-barked trunk. At all times of the year it is astonishingly attractive, especially when the trunk takes on striking colours of brown, gold, sienna, and red.

During December to February the Snow Gum flowers profusely, producing its white flowers in umbels of 3–7. The thick, usually lanceolate leaves, buds and fruits are often quite glaucous, giving a waxy appearance which adds to the attraction of the species.

Quite frequently on the high plains, areas of Snow Gum are burnt by bushfires. Many of the trees regenerate quite well from the base. Others, however, succumb, and after years of exposure to gales, blizzards, and associated elements, they become stark, weathered skeletons of their former selves. These grow white with age and stand like enormous trees of driftwood in the landscape, contrasting vividly, particularly in summer, with the dark green and brown surrounds of the vegetation of alpine Australia.

WHITE SALLY *E. pauciflora* subsp. *pauciflora* has a wider distribution and extends from New South Wales and Victoria to the south-east of South Australia, as well as Tasmania, where it is found at elevations, and also near sea-level. It can grow into quite a large, spreading tree.

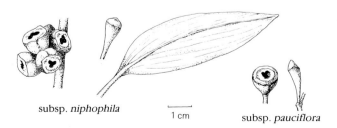

subsp. *niphophila*   1 cm   subsp. *pauciflora*

MOUNTAIN ASH

Eucalyptus regnans F. Muell.
MYRTACEAE

Mountain Ash is Australia's tallest tree, and one of the world's tallest, specimens having been found over 115 m in height.

It is a giant, shaft-like tree of the high-rainfall country of Victoria and Tasmania. In Victoria it is found in the mountains of the east with a restricted occurrence in the Otway Range, and in Tasmania in the north-east, the south-east, and the Huon and Derwent valleys.

Climate is cool to mild in summer with cold wet winters, and some snow in the higher altitude range. Annual rainfall is 750–1500 mm, most of which falls in winter.

The best trees are found in the mountain valleys in deep, rich, moist soils, usually in pure stands. A pure stand of these giants with an understorey of tree-ferns and ground cover shrubs is a sight to be long remembered by all lovers of the Australian bushland. On the poorer soils Mountain Ash occurs with other eucalypt species such as Messmate (*E. obliqua*, p.166).

Usual tree heights range from 50 to 80 m. The trunk is long and straight, up to 3 m in diameter at the base, with a sparse, open crown. The bark is rough and persistent at the base and up to 16 m, but smooth thereafter, white or pale grey in colour, and is shed in long ribbons, often up to 10 m in length, which hang from the trees. Adult leaves are long, narrow, and curved, and a smooth, shining green on both sides. The small white flowers bloom mainly in late summer.

Mountain Ash is one of Australia's most valuable timber trees. The timber is used extensively in joinery, furniture, and various structures, as well as in the pulping industry. Like that of Messmate, it is known as Australian Oak or Tasmanian Oak. It has a pale brown or cream-coloured open texture with a straight grain, is easily worked and dressed, and is hard and durable.

There has been little attempt to grow this species in Australia, except in State Forests.

1 cm

CANDLEBARK

Eucalyptus rubida Deane & Maiden
MYRTACEAE

At its best Candlebark is one of Australia's loveliest gum trees. Although it is more prevalent in the eastern States, some of the best specimens are seen in parts of the Mount Lofty Ranges near Adelaide. In the richer soils and in gullies near creeks, majestic specimens with gleaming white bark remain in solitary splendour, 35 m or more high, and perfect in every detail.

The tree is native to the cooler, hilly areas of New South Wales, Victoria, Tasmania, and South Australia where rainfall usually exceeds 750 mm and soils are alluvial or granite.

It can be a tall straight tree with an open crown and powdery white bark on the trunk and branches, or, often in poorer soils, a relatively small thick tree with a somewhat crooked, or leaning, trunk, and sometimes a multicoloured bark rather akin to that of the River Red Gum.

The trunk is 1 m or more in diameter with a smooth bark which peels off in flakes leaving the bole a pure white which darkens to a salmon pink before decorticating again.

Leaves are rather broad and pointed, glaucous in the juvenile stages, and often remaining so, or sometimes becoming a dull green when mature. Flowers are in axillary umbels of three, and are small and white. Timber is pink or red and worthless except for fuel.

This tree is best suited to cool, wet, elevated conditions in a temperate climate, where it makes a large specimen tree of striking beauty, particularly after the old bark has just been shed. It flowers in summer and is a good honey tree.

MANNA GUM *E. viminalis* Labill. subsp. *viminalis* is a closely related companion of the Candlebark. This is a tall forest tree that prefers cool mountain valleys and is found in all southern and eastern States. It is usually 35–50 m high; the long shaft-like trunk, 1–2 m in diameter, has rough, ribbony bark at the base, but is smooth and white above. Ribbony scaling bark often hangs in long strands from the upper branches. The tree has a fairly open crown, with rather drooping branchlets, and long narrow leaves.

This is an ornamental species suited to cool, mountainous situations.

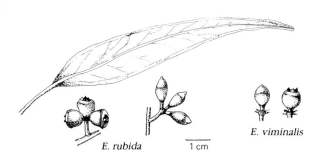

E. rubida

1 cm

E. viminalis

SALMON GUM

Eucalyptus salmonophloia F. Muell.
MYRTACEAE

Widespread throughout the eastern goldfields and agricultural areas of Western Australia, Salmon Gum extends from some distance east of the Norseman–Kalgoorlie area to a western limit about 160 km or so from Perth. Its northern limit is near Mullewa, and its southern limit, the Oldfield River to Salmon Gums.

The tree is found in open woodland usually on red, loamy, alkaline soils supporting an understorey of bluebush, *Acacia*, *Eremophila*, and other low-growing vegetation. Associated trees are mainly *Eucalyptus* species, such as Gimlet (*E. salubris*), Morrel (*E. gracilis*), and several others. Its presence has always been considered an indication of good soil well suited to agriculture, although it still remains a feature of the landscape in the 200–250 mm rainfall areas that are too dry for growing crops.

Salmon Gum is an exceptionally handsome, erect, and shapely tree growing up to 28 m high, with a long, smooth-barked trunk, and small rounded crown. Where single specimens have been allowed to remain in cleared areas, the tree is more wide-spreading, and gives ample shade.

The smooth bark, as with so many trees of the genus, is a feature of the tree. Light reddish brown when first exposed, it changes to a salmon pink in summer and then to pale grey or white before shedding in autumn to winter. Leaves, 7–12 cm long, are a deep lustrous green, and give the tree a burnished or lacquered effect. The small white flowers which occur in summer are rich in nectar, making the tree an excellent species for apiarists.

The roots of Salmon Gum are very shallow and wide-spreading.

This is a fine ornamental tree which should be more widely cultivated in dry areas.

DUNDAS MAHOGANY *E. brockwayi* C. Gardner is a tree of similar size and general appearance, found only in a restricted area near Norseman. It can be distinguished by its bark which is usually paler (although it is deep red when new), and its quite different, urn-shaped fruits.

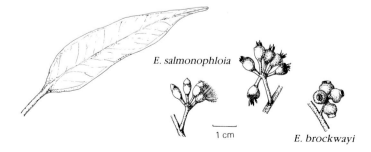

E. salmonophloia

E. brockwayi

1 cm

GIMLET GUM

Eucalyptus salubris F. Muell.
MYRTACEAE

The Gimlet Gum is one of the best-known and commonest trees of the Western Australian eastern agricultural and eastern goldfields districts. It has a distribution northwards as far as Mullewa, and southwards to the Ravensthorpe area.

The tree almost always inhabits rich red alkaline clay loams, often in open woodland association with Salmon Gum (*E. salmonophloia*). Rainfall is 200–500 mm. In the low-rainfall goldfields areas it is never stunted as might be expected, but is seen as a fine tree which, with Salmon Gum, and sometimes other eucalypts, dominates the landscape.

Gimlet Gum is easily recognised by its smooth, clean, varnished, red-brown to greenish brown bark, and often fluted or spirally twisted trunk, especially in the younger trees. Mature trees reach 28 m in height with usually an upright, regular habit, and a bushy, well-proportioned crown of glistening, dark green foliage. The upper branches are smooth and reddish in colour. Flowers are white and produced in axillary umbels, and the fruits are quite small. Flowering time is variable, from March to October.

SILVER-TOPPED GIMLET *E. campaspe* S. Moore is a closely related species confined to the eastern goldfields area of Western Australia.

It is a smaller tree, up to 12 m high, with a wide-spreading crown in solitary specimens, but where it grows in thickets — as it often does — the tree appears in a very slender, sparsely crowned, whipstick formation.

This tree is very easily distinguished from Gimlet by the whitish powder on the upper branches, and by the blue-green (glaucous) leaves. The fruits, also, are larger.

The pale brown timber of both gimlets is very, hard, durable, and straight-grained, and has been used extensively for tool handles, etc. The tree flowers in summer.

Both trees are adaptable, and extremely useful for both ornamental and shelter planting, particularly in dry areas. Silver-topped Gimlet is used as a street tree in inland towns.

E. salubris

1 cm

E. campaspe

WALLANGARRA WHITE GUM

Eucalyptus scoparia Maiden
MYRTACEAE

This lovely eucalypt is not common in the wild, being restricted to a localised habitat on the tops of granite hills around the town of Wallangarra and on both sides of the nearby border between New South Wales and Queensland.

Nevertheless, because of its ornamental appearance and usually moderate size, coupled with surprisingly rapid growth in its early years, Wallangarra White Gum has become increasingly well known as a cultivated tree suited to park and garden specimen planting.

At its best it rarely grows higher than 10–12 m with an erect, rather slender habit and extremely attractive long, narrow leaves which hang downwards in willow-like manner. The trunk is smooth and white, ageing to pale grey and white patches, and the leaves are a dark shining green; the whole effect is very ornamental.

The alternate linear-lanceolate leaves are normally about 20 cm long by 1–1·5 cm broad, with very faint venation. The small white flowers are borne in umbels of usually 3–7, appearing in summer, autumn, or winter, depending on the season. Bud caps are hemispherical with a short beak. The ovoid fruits have a prominent, raised hemispherical disc.

There are two forms of this species being cultivated. One has broader, less graceful foliage and is not quite so attractive in habit, but is a more vigorous and reliable tree under most conditions. It is the willowy form, however, which is sought after and this form, although sometimes unreliable in cultivation, normally is successful on well-drained soils with assured rainfall.

BRITTLE GUM *E. mannifera* Mudie ssp. *maculosa* (R. T. Baker) L. Johnson, a common white-trunked tree in and around Canberra, has very similar, slightly smaller buds and fruits, but can be distinguished by its shorter, stiffer leaves and general growth habit, which is not so willowy.

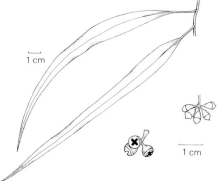

RED IRONBARK, MUGGA

Eucalyptus sideroxylon Cunn. ex Woolls
subsp. *sideroxylon*
MYRTACEAE

Red Ironbark is a medium-sized tree found commonly in undulating woodland extending from north central Victoria through the western slopes of the Great Dividing Range in New South Wales to southern Queensland. It is usually found in poor shallow soils with a 350–650 mm rainfall and temperate climate, except in the northern extremities of its range where it is subtropical. Associated trees include Yellow Box (*E. melliodora*), Yellow Gum (*E. leucoxylon*), Red Stringybark (*E. macrorhyncha*), and several other trees of the 'box' and 'ironbark' group.

There are also scattered occurrences in the higher-rainfall coastal areas of northern Victoria and southern New South Wales.

The 'ironbark' trees are a very distinctive group of Australian eucalypts, easily recognised by the hard, deeply furrowed, rough bark, which is dark grey or almost black in colour, and persists to the smaller branches. Foliage is usually a dull grey or grey-blue and provides a handsome contrast to the dark trunk. The timber is valued for its strength and durability, being hard and dense with an interlocked grain. In Red Ironbark the timber is a dark red colour.

Red Ironbark is a tree that can reach 33 m in height, but is usually much less, with a slender trunk of no significant height before the first branches appear.

A pink-flowered form is often planted for ornamental purposes. Particularly in its young stages, the combination of grey-blue foliage, black trunk, and showy small pink flowers, is extremely attractive.

It is an adaptable tree tolerating most soils, including limestone. Flowering time is usually late winter.

NARROW-LEAVED RED IRONBARK *E. crebra* F. Muell. and BROAD-LEAVED RED IRONBARK *E. fibrosa* F. Muell. subsp. *fibrosa* are somewhat similar trees of coastal Queensland and New South Wales. Narrow-leaved Red Ironbark has a particularly wide distribution extending along the coast from south of Sydney to north Queensland, and some 500 km inland to the dry western plains.

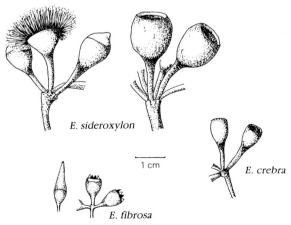

E. sideroxylon

1 cm

E. crebra

E. fibrosa

RED MALLEE

Eucalyptus socialis F. Muell. ex. Miq.
MYRTACEAE

This mallee is, with Giant Mallee (*E. oleosa*, p. 168), one of the most widely distributed mallee eucalypts in Australia. It is found throughout the mallee regions of all States except Western Australia, where the very closely related *E. transcontinentalis* grows in the goldfields and wheatbelt areas.

Red Mallee is variable in form, but is usually a multistemmed mallee, 5–8 m high, with a light canopy of greyish, or grey-blue, lanceolate leaves. Both leaves and twigs may be covered with a waxy bloom.

The bark is mainly smooth and pale grey with persistent rough bark at the base and red on the young branchlets.

Flowering, from winter to summer, can be profuse, the flowers being cream to a bright lemon colour, occurring in stalked umbels. The long yellowish bud caps, resembling an elf's cap, are a distinctive feature. Fruits are rounded or slightly urn-shaped, with long, pointed, protruding valves which soon fracture.

Red Mallee forms a useful and ornamental small tree which is easily grown in most conditions, including very alkaline limestone soils, where climate is temperate. It is drought-resistant, except in very arid situations.

REDWOOD or BOONGUL *E. transcontinentalis* Maiden is a much larger tree from Western Australia, usually forming a slender-trunked, erect tree 15–20 m high, with pale grey bark and greyish blue foliage. The flowers and fruits are virtually identical to those of *E. socialis*, but Redwood can be distinguished at the seedling stage, when the seedling leaves are broader and decurrent (i.e. forming a wing along the stem). This is a handsome slender tree which has not responded very well to cultivation. It flowers in the spring months.

Both species are excellent honey trees.

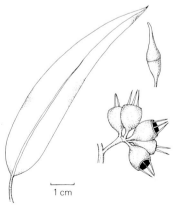

1 cm

CARBEEN, MORETON BAY ASH

Eucalyptus tessellaris F. Muell.
MYRTACEAE

Carbeen is one of the commonest trees of eastern Queensland, where it extends from the State's southern boundary (and just into northern New South Wales) to Cape York Peninsula. It can be seen growing almost to the water's edge along the coast, in the mountains, and further inland in the drier foothills to the west (usually in a more stunted form).

The tree is very easily recognised because of its characteristic bark. This comprises a short stocking of dark grey persistent bark which extends from the ground to several metres up and then changes abruptly to smooth, deciduous, cream or pale grey-green bark over the remainder of the tree. The short stocking of dark grey bark is cracked into small regular segments (tessellated), and it is from this that the tree's specific name is derived.

At its best Carbeen will grow to 20–25 m high with a straight, fairly slim trunk, and a drooping canopy of handsome, slender mid-green leaves. The new leaves, usually in winter, are a bright lettuce green and give the tree a fresh, ornamental appearance.

The creamy white flowers are normally borne in summer in attractive panicles. Bud caps are flatly conical or beret-shaped and the fruits cup-shaped, thin-walled and easily crushed. The leaves, too, are very thin and soft, and the twigs are brittle and easily broken.

Carbeen is essentially a tree of summer rainfall, very common in tropical eastern Queensland. It is found on a range of soil types but appears to favour those of sandy origin.

Despite its natural habitat it can be grown successfully as far south as Adelaide on the better soils, where it forms a very handsome, graceful tree of medium size, well suited to ornamental planting. It is a particularly ornamental tree in northern Queensland where it grows naturally and has been allowed to remain in parks and home sites.

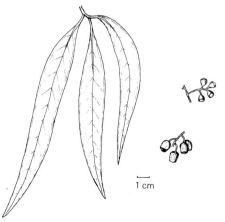

CORAL GUM, COOLGARDIE GUM

Eucalyptus torquata Luehm.

MYRTACEAE

Coral Gum has a restricted habitat in the Coolgardie–Norseman area of the eastern goldfields of Western Australia, and is far from common even there.

Because of its attractive flowers and shapely habit, however, it has rapidly become a popular and well-known species throughout the drier regions of Australia, where it is frequently cultivated, both as a garden and as a street tree.

This tree hybridises very freely and many garden cultivars with an affinity to Coral Gum are now being grown. In Kalgoorlie there are many examples of related trees in the streets, each with interesting and beautiful flower variations. One cultivar known as *E.* 'Torwood' is a variable tree, but almost always has large clusters of beautiful orange or orange-yellow flowers (see p. 192).

Under natural conditions Coral Gum is a shapely tree, 8–12 m high, with a dense, spreading crown of blue-green foliage. Its shapeliness under these conditions probably explains why it is so reliable when cultivated.

Bark is dark grey, almost black, rough, and persistent. The very decorative flowers hang in abundant pendulous clusters. They are usually a coral pink colour, but variations occur from creamy yellow to red. Flower buds are also very beautiful, being orange-yellow with a ribbed base and enclosed by an attractively shaped, ribbed operculum. These contrast very well with the bluish leaves. The tree blooms when very young, produces an abundance of nectar, and is an excellent tree for apiarists. It flowers from November to March.

Coral Gum is extremely reliable in cultivation provided rainfall is under about 600 mm and frosts are few, but is perhaps seen at its best where rainfall is as low as 200–250 mm. Flowers are usually more vivid under very dry conditions. It is not particular as regards soils.

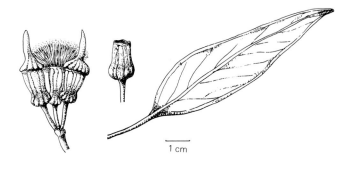

1 cm

TORWOOD

Eucalyptus × 'Torwood'
MYRTACEAE

This is a hybrid eucalypt with no real common name but often just referred to as 'Torwood' after its cultivar name, the tree originally being an accidental hybrid between Coral Gum (*E. torquata*, p. 190) and Lemon-flowered Gum (*E. woodwardii*).

Unfortunately, because of its popularity as a cultivated tree for mainly the drier areas, *E.* 'Torwood' has frequently been planted where further hybridisation could occur. As a consequence, seedling trees tend to be quite variable, particularly in regard to flower colour, which may vary from a vivid orange-yellow through various shades of yellows to, rarely, cream.

At its best this is a magnificent flowering tree, retaining the compact, but usually slightly more slender, form of *E. torquata*, and displaying over a long period from winter to summer, masses of bright orange to yellow flowers. These tend to resemble those of *E. torquata*, but are larger and more conspicuously clustered like the flowers of *E. woodwardii*. The photograph, taken in Hawker, South Australia, typifies this tree in flower. It is particularly suited to areas where summers are dry and rainfall is less than 400 mm annually, where it usually forms a neat, erect tree to 5–8 m high.

The broadly lanceolate or falcate leaves are thick and leathery, but not glaucous like those of *E. woodwardii*, and usually broader than those of *E. torquata*. As stated, the flowers and fruits are variable, but tend to retain the operculum of *E. torquata* and more or less the fruit shape of *E. woodwardii*. Bark, too, is variable, but never rough and fibrous like that of *E. torquata*.

LEMON-FLOWERED GUM *E. woodwardii* Maiden is quite different in appearance from the foregoing, being a very glaucous tree with long, flexuous branches, sometimes rather straggly in habit, powdery white flower buds and prolific clusters of cascading brilliant yellow flowers over long periods. It is found naturally in a restricted area of Western Australia, east of Kalgoorlie. However, it too is popularly cultivated although, because of its unreliable growth habit, it is really only suited to very dry inland areas, where it grows strongly enough to form a self-supporting, ornamental tree.

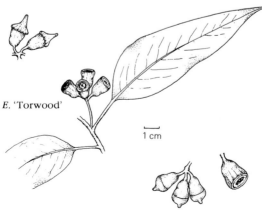

E. 'Torwood'

1 cm

E. woodwardii

PINK EVODIA, PINK-FLOWERED DOUGHWOOD

Euodia elleryana F. Muell.

RUTACEAE

Once known as *Evodia* (hence its common name), this is a small to medium-sized tree from the rainforests, where it is reported to extend from the Richmond River area in northern New South Wales to the Atherton Tableland in Queensland. It also occurs in Papua New Guinea and the Solomon Islands.

It is not a tree which is often noticed in its natural habitat, but it has won favour as an ornamental flowering tree for cultivation because of its very attractive pink or mauve flowers. These grow in thick clusters along the branches inside the tree's canopy and are well illustrated in the photograph opposite.

This tree is normally no more than 8–10 m high, supporting a well-balanced array of branches in pyramidal form and handsome deep, shiny green foliage, making it an excellent small shade tree for average gardens. Both the flowers and the fruits attract birds and the tree is the foodplant of the famous Blue Ulysses butterfly of the rainforests.

The leaflets of the compound leaves are in threes (trifoliolate), each leaflet normally about 12 cm long by 4–6 cm wide; the leaves themselves are arranged in opposite pairs on the branches. Flowers are borne in lateral cymes growing out of the previous season's wood; they are deep pink in colour, appearing in summer. The fruits which follow resemble clusters of deep green berries but split open to reveal the small, dark reddish brown, egg-shaped seeds. These self-sow very readily and young seedlings can frequently be found beneath a mature tree.

Pink Evodia appears to be the only species of the genus that is cultivated and that has become well known in Australia, although about twelve species have been recorded all from the east coast rainforests.

This is an ornamental, small tree in cultivation, one which can be readily grown in warm, frost-free areas where moisture is assured. It is a successful garden tree in Brisbane.

fruits

opened fruit
(enlarged)

2 cm

NATIVE CHERRY

Exocarpos cupressiformis Labill.
SANTALACEAE

Throughout the wetter parts of temperate Australia, particularly in hilly country, the conifer-like Native Cherry commands attention wherever it is encountered. This tree with its cypress-like foliage, often faintly golden in appearance, contrasts conspicuously with the more sombre greens of the dominant eucalypt and other associated plants of this terrain.

It belongs to the sandalwood family, and in common with most of these plants, is a root parasite, but does not appear to harm the plants from which it feeds. Regenerating freely from root suckers, it is often seen in closely grouped clumps, particularly on road banks where land clearing has missed the native vegetation.

The tree is dense, with a coniferous habit, usually 4–8 m high. The slender branches are covered with rough, scabrous grey bark, and the foliage, which consists of leaves reduced to scales, resembles the garden cypress in appearance, and is pale green to golden green in colour.

The minute and inconspicuous flowers are produced on stiff, green stalks (peduncles) which swell to a brightly coloured, rounded, cone- or pear-shaped receptacle, which is succulent and edible. These are surmounted by a smaller hard green fruit at the tip of the fleshy receptacle. At about Christmas time they are very decorative when they ripen, and colours on any one tree at the same time vary from green, through yellow and orange, to a bright red.

This lovely little tree should be preserved wherever possible on properties, and is well worth attempts to cultivate it as a specimen tree.

There are about twenty species of *Exocarpos*, all native to the Southern Hemisphere. Apart from Native Cherry, those endemic to Australia are mainly only shrubby in stature. *Exocarpos sparteus* R. Br. is usually only a single-stemmed shrub, but sometimes a small tree to 5 m with long, weeping, broom-like foliage of a pale golden green colour. It is often seen growing at the base of larger trees where it forms a distinctive and lovely bush plant.

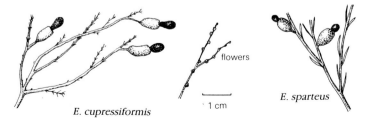

E. cupressiformis

flowers

1 cm

E. sparteus

MORETON BAY FIG

Ficus macrophylla Desf. ex Pers.
MORACEAE

Moreton Bay Fig is a massive tree inhabiting the rainforests of coastal northern New South Wales to northern Queensland, and inland to the Bunya Mountains.

Most species of *Ficus* are large to gigantic trees belonging to the tropical rainforests of mainly Queensland. Under these conditions, the seeds of some species are lodged in the branches of associated trees where they germinate and send down aerial roots which eventually strangle the host tree on which they began their life.

The genus is distinguished by the fruit (fig), which consists of a fleshy receptacle containing minute flowers on the inner surface. Additionally, the branches and leaf stalks, when cut, exude a sticky white juice. Several species are very similar in general appearance, particularly when cultivated as park trees, when they form dense, spreading trees which branch to the ground, and cover an area often greater in diameter than their height.

Under forest conditions Moreton Bay Fig attains a height of 50 m. It has a thick buttressed trunk and massive spreading roots often partly visible above the ground. The bark is grey and rough, and the leaves are large, about 20 cm long by 8 cm broad, dark glossy green, and leathery. The undersurface is brownish-coloured and displays the vein structure quite prominently. The young buds are protected by stipules which are folded around them and taper to a long point. Fruits are globular, purple dotted white, and about 2·5 cm in diameter, on thick stalks.

Once extensively planted by the early settlers, who apparently recognised the need for shade trees of this type, Moreton Bay Fig is seldom cultivated today. There are many parts of Australia with hot, dry summers where it is easily grown, and where there could hardly be a better tree for park planting. Today the tree is more often grown in pots and used in its seedling stage as a successful indoor plant.

GREEN-LEAVED MORETON BAY FIG *F. watkinsiana* Bailey is found in similar localities and is very like Moreton Bay Fig in appearance. Its leaves, however, are green on both surfaces, and the purple fruits have a distinct nipple at the apex.

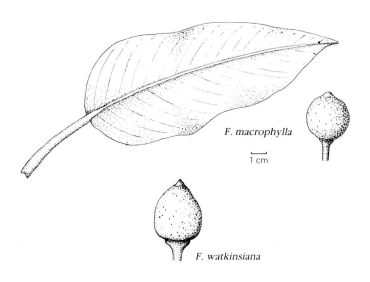

F. macrophylla

1 cm

F. watkinsiana

RUSTY-LEAVED FIG, PORT JACKSON FIG

Ficus rubiginosa Desf. ex Vent.
MORACEAE

Rusty-leaved Fig is a very large tree which is restricted to New South Wales and Queensland, being found in the rainforests extending from south of Batemans Bay to the Darling Downs, where it occurs in isolated areas.

Apart from the Moreton Bay Fig, this tree is perhaps the most commonly seen native fig in cultivation, and grows quite easily in relatively harsh, but frost-free, conditions. It is easily distinguished from the former by its leaves, which are smaller and more round in shape with a velvet rust-coloured undersurface. However, under natural conditions this tree is quite variable in general form and in the amount of rusty tomentum on the foliage.

When cultivated this tree usually does not attain the massive proportions of the Moreton Bay Fig, but under natural conditions it is a tree of similar stature. Here it reaches a height of 50 m with a large buttressed trunk over 2 m in diameter. The bark is grey, and the thick branchlets are hairy. Leaves are elliptical with a blunt point at the apex, dark green and glossy on top, but rusty and hairy underneath. The leaf stalks, too, are covered with fine hairs. Fruits are oval-shaped, often bluntly pointed, 1–2 cm in diameter, and dotted.

Rusty-leafed Fig forms a handsome spreading shade tree up to 20 m in height, well suited for planting in parks and golf courses throughout most settled parts of Australia.

A variegated form of this tree, *F. rubiginosa* 'Variegata' is used extensively as a pot and tub plant. When planted for ornament it forms a dense, conical tree of handsome appearance.

SMALL-LEAVED FIG *F. obliqua* Forst. f. (syn. *F. eugenioides* F. Muell.) is a Queensland species that is scattered throughout many rainforest scrubs of that State. In general appearance it resembles the Rusty-leaved Fig, although the leaves are smaller and more pointed, smooth, and paler green on both surfaces. Fruits are small and globular, yellow when ripe.

This tree has been successfully grown as a street tree in Whyalla, South Australia, where soil is dry and very alkaline, and rainfall usually under 300 mm.

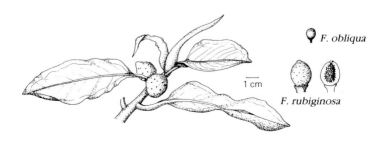

F. obliqua

1 cm

F. rubiginosa

CROW'S ASH,
AUSTRALIAN TEAK

Flindersia australis R. Br.

RUTACEAE

Crow's Ash is a fairly common member of the *Flindersia* genus which, with two exceptions, are large subtropical or tropical rainforest trees of Queensland, and in some cases New South Wales, usually growing well over 35 m tall.

The genus commemorates Captain Matthew Flinders and belongs to the same family (Rutaceae) as several of Australia's choice dwarf shrubs, such as *Boronia*, *Correa*, *Eriostemon*, etc. There are twenty-one recorded species of *Flindersia*, fourteen of these being Australian. As is the case with several other rainforest genera, odd species are found in dry areas of the continent. In this case, Leopard Wood (*F. maculosa*, p.204) and *F. strzeleckiana* F. Muell. are dry area species.

The rainforest *Flindersia* species are mainly fine timber trees and include the popular and much-used Queensland Maple (*F. brayleyana* F. Muell.) found in the Atherton district near Cairns. Crow's Ash timber is also used extensively in the building industry.

Crow's Ash is a tall, upright, semideciduous tree growing up to 50 m high with a scaly, brown bark on a trunk up to 1·5 m in diameter.

The handsome, pinnate leaves comprise egg-shaped or elliptical leaflets arranged in opposite pairs, with a single leaflet at the tip. These are dark green, paler underneath, with numerous minute, transparent dots which are prominent when held to the light. Flowers are small and white with a brown centre, and occur in dense terminal panicles in spring months.

The hard, woody fruits, which remain united at the base, open to expose four, five or six valves containing flat, winged seeds. The attractively shaped fruit covered with blunt spines when dried forms a fine subject for interior decoration or floral art work.

Many of the rainforest trees, in their search for light, grow tall and shaft-like under natural conditions, but are lower and more spreading when cultivated as single specimens, particularly in the cooler southern climates. Crow's Ash, however, retains its tall forest habit under these conditions also, and is usually too large for average gardens. It requires rich, moist soils.

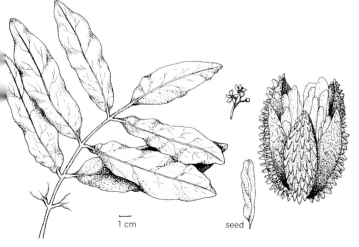

1 cm   seed

LEOPARD WOOD

Flindersia maculosa Benth.
RUTACEAE

Leopard Wood is a dry area tree belonging to a genus of mainly tropical rainforest species. It is found in the low-rainfall areas of north-west New South Wales, extending from near Broken Hill to the western slopes of the Great Dividing Range, and in Queensland, often in association with Wilga (*Geijera parviflora*).

Areas dominated by Leopard Wood are usually only lightly wooded, very often on elevated red sandy soils with an understorey of saltbush and other associated species. It is also found on heavy soils, although it favours the deep sands in which it grows best.

A curious feature of the tree is its manner of growth in the early stages of its life. Beginning as a tangled mass of long thin branches, it eventually produces a leading shoot which is protected by the tangled branches as it develops to a straight main stem.

Eventually a graceful medium-sized tree to 14 m in height is formed. It has a single trunk with handsome spotted or mottled bark, the mottled effect being caused by the outer layers falling off in patches. The narrow, opposite leaves are 2–7 cm long, occasionally lobed. Flowers are cream, in terminal panicles, individually small but occurring in showy masses in spring. Fruit is a hard capsule, 2·5–4 cm long, and containing flat seeds, winged at each end.

The yellow-coloured timber has a tough grain but is only useful for indoor use as it deteriorates rapidly when exposed. A pleasant-tasting, amber-coloured gum is exuded in quite large quantities in summer, and this can be made into an excellent adhesive mucilage. The foliage is sometimes used as fodder in times of drought, but the tree is not generally considered a good fodder tree.

Leopard Wood is a very ornamental, but seldom cultivated tree which would probably succeed on many soil types where drainage is good.

seed

1 cm

WILGA

Geijera parviflora Lindl.
RUTACEAE

Wilga is a delightful little tree from the dry areas, found mainly on the western plains of New South Wales and Queensland, but also in northern South Australia and north-west Victoria, often in sandy soils.

The tree is loved by stock, which frequently nibble the lower foliage, producing a very formal effect among natural trees. A stand of Wilga are sometimes the only trees to be seen in an arid landscape. Displayed in this way they are quite striking. Herbivores unfortunately eat many of the young plants before they are able to develop and in some areas the tree has become quite rare.

Wilga is usually low-growing, 5–8 m high, and of symmetrical outline, with a dense, rounded crown often wider than its over-all height, drooping grey foliage, and a short upright trunk. Bark is dark grey to brown.

The long, narrow, linear leaves are pleasantly aromatic when crushed. Flowers are bell-shaped, small, and white, usually appearing in winter in loose panicles which combine with the grey foliage to create a lovely silvery effect. Fruiting carpels are small and globular, containing hard, shiny, black seeds.

There are few examples of this tree in cultivation, although in Adelaide, at least, specimens are occasionally encountered. It is fairly slow-growing, but deep-rooted and permanent, and its ideal shape makes it an excellent tree for planting under overhead service wires, either in the street or elsewhere.

Geijera is an entirely Australian genus, and is limited to five species.

SCRUB WILGA *Geijera salicifolia* Schott is quite a large, upright rainforest tree growing to 28 m, from the brush forests of New South Wales and Queensland. The bark is rough and scaly and the leaves are lance-shaped and usually broad, but a narrow-leaved form also occurs. The timber is useful for various purposes.

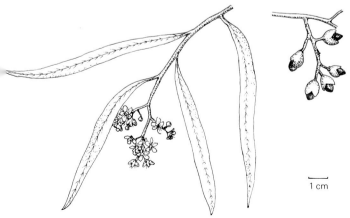

1 cm

CHEESE TREE

Glochidion ferdinandii (F. Muell.) F. M. Bailey
EUPHORBIACEAE

The Cheese Tree is a member of a very large, diverse and perhaps confused family. There are fifteen recorded species of
Glochidion in Australia, the genus being distinguished by the
male flowers, which are without discs but carry erect or
depressed, more or less united styles.

This particular species is fairly common along the warm east
coast regions of central and northern New South Wales, but
extends from the Illawarra district to north Queensland and
north-west Australia, as well as tropical Asia. It is often seen
growing in the most inhospitable places after the seed has been
spread by birds.

At its best the tree may grow to 25 m but, like most trees of
the rainforests, it is seldom more than a small to medium-sized
tree to 10 m high when cultivated. It is densely branched with
a good canopy of glossy green foliage which deciduates in late
spring (in Adelaide). The handsome entire leaves are alternate
in two rows, giving the appearance of pinnate foliage. They are
broadly lanceolate, usually 6–8 cm long by about 2·5 cm wide,
glossy on the upper surface, with prominent main veins. New
foliage is an attractive pink.

The small, five-petalled, unisexual flowers, which occur in
the forks of the leaves, are inconspicuous and cream-coloured,
the female ones solitary and the males in clusters.

It is the bumpy but smooth fruits which give the common
name to this tree, supposedly resembling small Dutch cheeses
in shape, although they are perhaps more like miniature pump-
kins. They are reddish when ripe, comprising five to seven dual
cells with two orange seeds in each. Each fruit is 1·5 to 2 cm
across.

The soft red timber is close-grained and easily worked but is
not used much in the timber industry.

In cultivation, the tree is an easily grown, hardy and
ornamental tree. In areas such as Brisbane and the moist east
coast regions it is fast-growing, but it is much slower in the
cooler southern areas such as Adelaide where it can be grown
successfully.

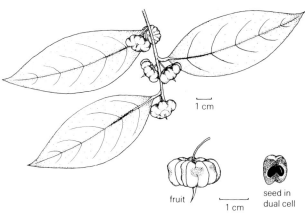

fruit

seed in
dual cell

1 cm

1 cm

WHITE BEECH, GREY TEAK

Gmelina lcichhardtii (F. Muell.) F. Muell. ex Benth.

VERBENACEAE

A tall, semideciduous tree from the coastal scrub forests of the east coast, White Beech is found from the Shoalhaven River south of Sydney, to Rockingham Bay near Tully in north Queensland. Owing to the demand for its timber it is no longer very prevalent in these areas. Limited to only five Australian species, the genus consists mainly of plants native to tropical Asia, India, and Indonesia.

Under natural rainforest conditions White Beech reaches a height of 40 m with trunk diameter up to 1·5 m. Bark is grey and scaly. The handsome, opposite leaves, which are broadly ovate in shape, drop in November, the new leaves appearing soon after. Flowering occurs at this time. On the undersides of the leaves there is a prominent raised network of veins covered with a brown velvety down of fine hairs. This down persists to the young shoots, smaller branchlets, leaf stalks, and flowers.

The fully pedunculate tubular flowers are white with blue or violet and yellow markings in the throat, and are borne conspicuously above the foliage in large terminal panicles in summer. Fruits are succulent berries, purplish mauve in colour when ripe, flat-spherical in shape and enclosing a four-celled, hard stone which contains a small oval seed in each cell.

The durable timber is valued for many indoor purposes, being easy to work, with an attractive close grain.

White Beech is rarely seen in cultivation, but forms an attractive small specimen tree in drier, cooler climates, and is best suited to a well-drained, moist soil.

Apart from White Beech only one other species of *Gmelina* is found solely in Australia.

NORTH QUEENSLAND WHITE BEECH *G. fasciculiflora* Benth. is found only in north Queensland from Rockingham Bay to the Daintree River district. It is superficially very similar in general character to White Beech but is distinguished by the flowers, which are in sessile cymes forming panicles, and the globular fruits.

The other three species are also found outside Australia from New Guinea to Asia.

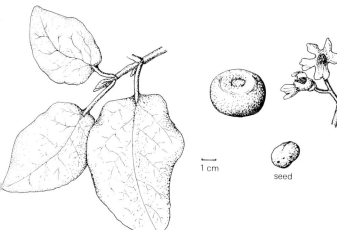

1 cm

seed

BUSHMAN'S CLOTHES PEG, CLOTHES PEG GREVILLEA

Grevillea glauca J. Knight
PROTEACEAE

This northern grevillea is very easily identified by its large, hard, woody, rounded fruits, which are unusual in a grevillea, and are usually present, if not on the tree, on the ground beneath it. The fruits partly open in a wedge-like manner and were allegedly used in the past by bushmen as clothes pegs, hence the common name.

This tree is native to northern Queensland from south of Cairns to Cooktown, both in sandy soils very near the shoreline and inland, mainly on the drier western slopes of the tablelands on a range of soil types.

The tree is only small, seldom higher than about 6 m, with a slender dark, almost black, trunk — the trunk and branches being clothed in rough, furrowed bark — and a distinctive canopy of light grey or silvery leaves. New foliage is an attractive silvery bronze. The leaves are elliptical to lanceolate, 7–15 cm long by 2·5 cm broad, and usually very undulate (fluted). Venation is very faint, parallel and at a sharp angle to the midrib.

Inflorescences are cylindrical racemes, up to 12 cm or so long, which droop in catkin fashion, rather like the flower heads of the *Macadamia* tree (p. 248). They are white and numerous, appearing in winter months.

The large hakea-like fruits have already been described above, each containing only one seed, which, unusually for a grevillea, is reluctantly released.

Bushman's Clothes Peg is not often cultivated, although it is grown in Townsville and can be seen growing naturally in urban areas of Port Douglas. It is quite an ornamental tree suited to small gardens, at least in areas of warm winters. The author has no knowledge of its cultivation potential in the cooler areas of Australia.

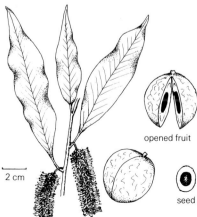

opened fruit

seed

2 cm

WATER BUSH

Grevillea nematophylla F. Muell.
PROTEACEAE

Water Bush is a small inland tree or tall shrub from the dry parts of Western Australia, South Australia, and, rarely, New South Wales. Although seldom exceeding 5–7 m in height, it often gives the impression of very great age with its gnarled shape and deeply fissured brown bark. It grows under many varying conditions, but is often seen at its best in light, sandy soils.

The genus *Grevillea* is an important member of the Australian flora, containing many beautiful flowering plants which range in size from dwarf undershrubs to (in a few instances) large forest trees. Most species bear quaint and beautiful, brightly coloured flowers, often over a long period, and are very decorative in the garden. The genus differs from the closely allied *Hakea* in its flat seeds which are shed each year after flowering, and its shell-like seed follicle. However, *G. glauca* (p. 212) differs in this regard, bearing large, woody fruits similar to those of the hakeas. Of the nearly 200 recorded species, only a very few are found outside Australia.

This particular species grows erect with upright branches and usually a narrow head of foliage during its early life. The leaves are long and slender, silvery grey in colour, and rather rigid. A tree in full flower in early summer is a magnificent sight with its masses of greenish cream flowers in dense racemes, produced mainly towards the ends of the branches. These are full of nectar and loved by birds and bees. Seed follicles which follow are dark brown when ripe, and about 1 cm across; they contain two flat seeds.

Easily grown from seed, this tree thrives in the drier cities such as Adelaide and many country towns, but is rarely seen in cultivation.

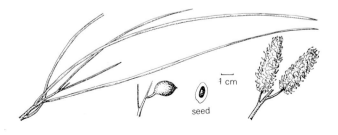

seed

1 cm

SILVER OAK

Grevillea parallela J. Knight
PROTEACEAE

Silver Oak is a widely distributed tree across the monsoonal regions of northern Australia, where it extends from the Kimberleys in Western Australia across the Northern Territory to northern Queensland, where it is common on the drier table-lands around Mareeba. It generally occurs in scrubby woodland or open forest in association with eucalypts and can go unnoticed because of its habit of often growing only as a stick-like shrub with little spread or foliage.

Even at its best this is only a small tree, up to 8 m high, and usually of slender habit. The trunk is slim, covered with dark, rough and furrowed bark. The leaves, however, are very hand-some, being long and slender, up to 30 cm long by 3–5 mm across, and pendulous, with a silvery undersurface from which the tree's common name is derived. The leaves are alternate and linear, with recurved margins and three distinct parallel veins on the undersurface.

The creamy white flowers are borne from June to October, in terminal racemes about 10 cm long. These are attractive but not as conspicuous as those of some of the other grevilleas. Fruits are follicles, 1·5–2 cm in diameter, with a thin beak. The seeds are surrounded by a membranous wing.

The timber of this small tree has a decorative oak grain and is durable under exposure.

A closely related species, *G. coriacea* McGillivray, grows in association with *G. parallela* in places, but can be distinguished by its stiffer, leathery, upright, and generally wider but shorter, green leaves with a distinct midrib on the undersurface. Its inflorescences are very similar, but perhaps slightly larger, often occurring slightly earlier than those of *G. parallela*.

The author has no knowledge of these species as cultivated plants, although both have some potential in areas of humid and wet summers, with mild winters. *Grevillea parallela* is recorded as growing on a range of soil types in areas where the rainfall is 700–1700 mm.

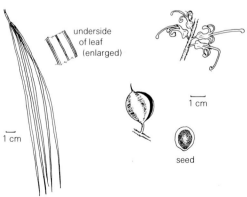

underside
of leaf
(enlarged)

1 cm

1 cm

seed

FERN-LEAVED GREVILLEA, ABERGUBBER

Grevillea pteridifolia J. Knight
PROTEACEAE

One of the loveliest flowering trees of northern Australia, Fern-leaved Grevillea is an inhabitant of the monsoonal areas, often found along the edges of freshwater swamps or streams, or on sandy soils. It is fairly widespread throughout tropical Western Australia, the Northern Territory, and Queensland.

Only a small tree, up to about 8 m high, it usually has a single trunk, and spreading, rather erect branches. In some ways it resembles the Silky Oak (*G. robusta*, p. 220), but it is much smaller, and has a more open habit of growth.

A feature of the tree is its large fern-like foliage, consisting of pinnate leaves made up of long linear segments, 15–20 cm in length, and very ornamental. Typically silvery grey, although the coastal form from parts of Queensland is much greener, this foliage combines with the flower spikes to produce a lovely effect.

Borne over a long period throughout the 'dry' season, the flowers are spectacular. They are carried in large, terminal racemes resembling very showy, rich orange spikes or cones. They are full of nectar which is sometimes used by the Aboriginals as nourishment.

Fruits or follicles are roundish in shape, and about 2 cm long.

A glorious sight in full flower, this tree is one of the very best tree grevilleas, and should be extensively cultivated, at least in tropical gardens, where it is known to be very hardy. Little is known of its adaptability to the cooler climates of the south.

Several other species of *Grevillea* are noted for their similar beautiful orange or flame-like flowers.

RUSH-LEAF GREVILLEA *G. juncifolia* Hook. is an inland tree up to 7 m high, with much to commend it as an ornamental flowering tree for dry conditions. It has long, erect, needle-like leaves, and masses of orange-yellow flowers in spring.

FLAME GREVILLEA *G. eriostachya* Lindl. (syn. *G. excelsior* Diels), common in the southern sand plains of Western Australia, is usually only a tall, very thin, pine-like shrub, or sometimes a tree growing to 7 m. From October to January the orange flower spikes are prolific and spectacular.

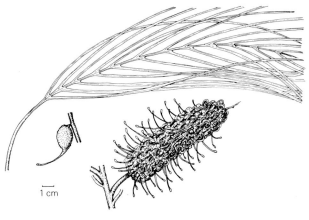

1 cm

SILKY OAK

Grevillea robusta Cunn. ex R. Br.
PROTEACEAE

Well known for both ornament and timber, Silky Oak is an inhabitant of the rainforests extending from the Clarence River in New South Wales to Maryborough and inland to the Bunya Mountains in Queensland. Valued for its distinctive silky-textured timber, the tree has now become quite rare in its natural state.

It is, however, frequently planted in streets, parks, and gardens, and is seen in many parts of Australia where frosts are not severe. At its best it is an erect, pyramidal tree, 30–40 m high, with a dark brown or grey, rough-barked trunk, about 1 m in diameter. Bark is furrowed and fissured, with a corky outer layer. The graceful, fern-like foliage is made up of large, doubly pinnate leaves, the individual leaflets divided into narrow lobes. Flowers usually come in early summer, when they appear as large, spectacular racemes of brush-like blooms, a bright cadmium yellow in colour. Fruits are boat-shaped follicles with a slender beak, about 2 cm long, and containing flat, oval-shaped seeds.

Silky Oak grows rapidly from seed, seldom exceeding 16 m in height when cultivated. It forms a fine, ornamental specimen tree best suited to rich, moist soils in warm situations, but is adaptable.

WHITE SILKY OAK *G. hilliana* F. Muell. is a somewhat smaller tree of the same areas but found as far north as Cairns in Queensland. It occasionally grows to nearly 33 m but is more usually only about half this height. This is also an upright forest tree with large glossy leaves, usually over 15 cm long, entire or deeply lobed, with a silky white undersurface. The long, white flowers are borne in numerous axillary racemes. Fruits are egg-shaped follicles.

The timber of this tree is beautifully figured, hard and heavy, and dresses and polishes well, resembling that of the Scrub Beefwood (see p. 296) in appearance. This too is an ornamental tree particularly suited to warm climates.

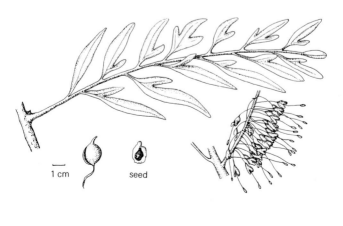

1 cm   seed

BEEFWOOD

Grevillea striata R. Br.
PROTEACEAE

Beefwood is a tree of extensive distribution within arid Australia, occurring over a wide range of Queensland where it extends to the drier tablelands not far from the coast, New South Wales, northern South Australia, and the drier southern half of the Northern Territory as well as Western Australia. The tree favours the heavier soils which are subjected to flooding, but is not confined to these conditions.

Beefwood owes its common name to the colour of the heartwood when freshly cut.

It is a small to medium-sized tree, 6–13 m high, often of handsome appearance, featuring narrow, strap-like foliage and a stout, rough-barked trunk. In sunlight, the silvery shimmer of the grey-green foliage enhances the beauty of this well-known tree.

Leaves are flat and leathery, broadly linear, and long — up to 45 cm — but usually no more than 0·5–0·7 cm wide. They are characterised by many fine longitudinal nerves (striae) from which the specific name is derived. The young growth is silky-hoary.

Creamy yellow erect flower spikes, 5–8 cm long, are produced abundantly at irregular periods, depending on seasons. These comprise numerous individual flowers arranged around a central stalk to form a raceme.

The fruiting follicles are broadly ovoid with an erect beak, about 1·5 cm long, containing two flat, oval seeds.

Beefwood timber is very durable when in contact with soil, a feature which has promoted its popularity in the inland for fence posts and other construction work. The resin was used by Aboriginals in the manufacture of implements.

Rarely cultivated, the tree could be used for ornamental planting in areas of hot summers, although it is slow growing. The foliage is eaten by stock and is of moderate nutritional value.

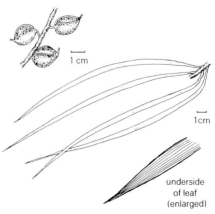

1 cm

1cm

underside
of leaf
(enlarged)

PINCUSHION HAKEA

Hakea laurina R. Br.

PROTEACEAE

Native only to parts of the south coast and some sand plain areas 160 km or so inland in Western Australia, Pincushion Hakea is seldom seen growing naturally, and where it is encountered it is usually only a slender shrub rarely reaching small tree size. It is better known in cultivation, where, under favourable conditions, it can form a dense, spreading tree 5–8 m high. Even when it remains shrubby it is usually densely branched and rounded in habit.

The genus *Hakea* is limited to Australia, with more than 100 species being found throughout the continent. These are all evergreens, mainly shrubs, though a few attain small tree proportions. They are distinguished by their hard woody fruits, each of which contains two black winged seeds. It is only these fruits that make it possible to distinguish some species from the genus *Grevillea*, to which they are closely related.

Pincushion Hakea is much loved for its flowers, which appear in autumn and winter. These form globular inflorescences, about the size of a golf ball, bright red or pink in colour, and covered with protruding cream styles like short pins. An all-red colour form also occurs. The flower buds are contained in bracts which peel off as the flower opens, each stage of opening being very beautiful, and adding interest to the overall effect.

The leaves resemble those of many of the eucalypt species but with prominent longitudinal nerves. When making new growth the young tips are a lovely, silky, golden bronze colour, and the old leaves assume bright colours prior to falling.

GRASS-LEAFED HAKEA *H. francisiana* F. Muell. is an inland species from South Australia and Western Australia favouring well-drained sandy soils. A tall shrub or small tree to 7 m with upright foliage, it has long, narrow, striate leaves, and prominent clusters of pink, red, or cream flower spikes produced over a long period in late winter and spring, often blooming twice in one season.

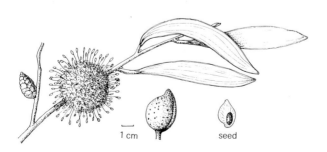

1 cm   seed

CORK-BARK TREE

Hakea suberea S. Moore
PROTEACEAE

Cork-bark Tree, a rather grotesque but fascinating species, is native to arid central Australia, where it is a conspicuous feature of the landscape. Usually twisted and contorted, often in fantastic attitudes, these trees command attention wherever they are seen. Resembling in some ways large bonsai trees, they have great appeal for both the tourist and the plant-lover.

At maturity, the tree is only 5–8 m high, with usually a rather sparse, but occasionally a dense, head of foliage. Bark is dark brown, very rough, and cork-like, and the trunk often thick and twisted. The leaves are terete, and up to 60 cm long, grey or grey-green in colour, and usually covered with a whitish tomentum.

The flowers are in large, torch-like spikes, cream or yellow in colour, and sweetly scented. They are loaded with honey which is much relished by the Aboriginals of these areas. An old tree in full flower is a wonderful sight, usually in winter or early spring.

At all times the Cork-bark Tree has an attraction all of its own, its ancient appearance suggesting hardiness and longevity.

SMALL-LEAVED CORK-BARK *H. divaricata* L. Johnson (syn. *H. intermedia* Ewart & Davies). This species is similar in appearance to Cork-bark Tree but has a denser crown of foliage which is not covered with a whitish grey tomentum. The leaves are short and divided, an olive green in colour. Flowers are similar but greenish. This tree is often found growing in association with *H. suberea*, but it has a less grotesque habit. It is fairly widespread throughout central Australia.

H. ivoryi Bailey is another inland tree in this group which reaches 10 m high, with deeply fissured bark, pungent needle-like leaves and attractive racemes of greenish cream flowers in spring.

NEEDLE HAKEA *H. leucoptera* R. Br. is another dry area species from south and eastern Australia which reaches small tree proportions. The long, pungent, needle-like leaves are an attractive hoary grey, and the flowers white, borne in prolific axillary racemes.

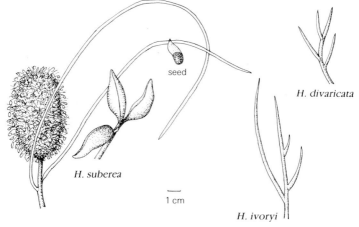

seed

H. suberea

H. divaricata

H. ivoryi

1 cm

TULIPWOOD

Harpullia pendula Planch. ex F. Muell.
SAPINDACEAE

Tulipwood is a dense evergreen tree from the coastal scrubs of northern New South Wales and Queensland as far north as Cairns, often found in sandy soils near the sea.

It is fairly extensively cultivated, particularly as a street tree in the warm, subtropical to tropical climates of many Queensland cities, and to a lesser extent in New South Wales. The tree grows quite well as far south as Adelaide but is rarely seen in plantings in that city.

In its natural forest environment Tulipwood reaches a height of 28 m, with a trunk 60 cm in diameter, sometimes buttressed at the base. When cultivated it is much shorter and more spreading, with a dense, shapely crown, and smooth grey bark which is shed in flakes. Leaves are alternate, and pinnate, consisting of 3–8 glossy, bright green leaflets, narrowly elliptical in shape. The young shoots are downy, and an attractive reddish brown in colour.

The flowers, which are borne in narrow panicles in the leaf axils, are comparatively inconspicuous, but are followed by bright orange fruits which are the colourful feature of the tree. These split open to reveal one or two jet black, shiny, round seeds, providing a pleasing contrast to the orange fruits. The fruits are variable both in the time of cropping and in the quantity produced. A tree that bears well is a beautiful sight.

Tulipwood is a shapely evergreen with handsome foliage that makes it particularly suitable for ornamental planting. It is well suited to street planting as it is relatively pest-free, and does not produce troublesome roots. In addition, the tree's natural habit of growth produces many twiggy small branchlets which make it easy to control with regular, light pruning.

It prefers rich, moist soils, and is fairly slow growing, at least when planted in climates cooler than its natural environment.

The heavy, close-grained, dark brown and yellow timber is attractive and useful, but is no longer very plentiful.

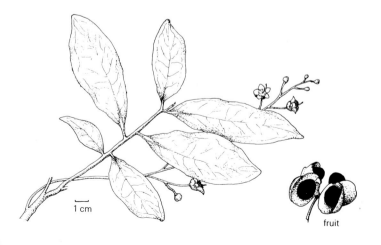

1 cm

fruit

BULLOCK BUSH, ROSEWOOD

Heterodendrum oleaefolium Desf.

SAPINDACEAE

A very widespread species from the dry parts of temperate Australia, Bullock Bush can be seen growing in many varying situations from sand dunes to deep-soil areas, and from rocky slopes to open plain country. It is a small tree native to all States except Tasmania.

The conspicuous features of this tree are its blue-green to silvery grey foliage, and its often contorted habit of growth which adds to its attractiveness in the landscape. Seldom more than 5–7 m high, it can be a single- or multi-stemmed tree with several joined, crooked, thick main stems. The rough bark on the trunk and branches is thick, dark brown, and deeply fissured. In appearance it closely resembles the bark of two frequently associated trees, Sugarwood (*Myoporum platycarpum*) and Long-leaved Emu Bush (*Eremophila longifolia*).

The tree is heavily canopied with olive-like leaves, 5–10 cm long and covered with an adpressed hoariness, which gives it its characteristic greyish appearance. Flowers are small and somewhat bell-shaped, without petals, green or yellow in colour, and carried in short, dense panicles in summer. The peculiar fruits are made up of 1–4 globular lobes, each containing one black shiny seed.

Timber is hard and dark brown but of no special importance.

The foliage is valued as cattle fodder, and this is probably the reason why the tree is on the list of South Australia's protected plants. Even so, stock are sometimes poisoned by eating the foliage of Bullock Bush, usually from young plants, and care should be taken to supplement it with other feed.

Good specimens of this tree are ornamental, and it can easily be pruned to produce a shapely, effective shade and shelter tree. Occasionally one sees Bullock Bush resembling a bonsai tree, and it is then that the attraction of this often overlooked plant is fully appreciated.

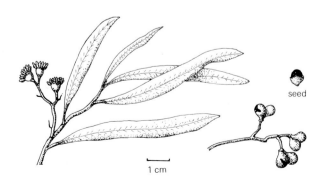

seed

1 cm

COTTONWOOD, COTTON TREE, MAHOE

Hibiscus tileaceus L.

MALVACEAE

Cottonwood can often be seen growing along the banks of rivers and streams in the warmer east and north coast regions of Australia from the Gulf of Carpentaria to the Gold Coast area of Queensland.

It is normally a dense, spreading tree of low stature to about 6 m high, often with its lower branches sprawling along the ground, or trailing into water. These can be trimmed and the tree trained to form a small, single-trunked tree, useful for street and park planting near the sea. In wet situations its lower branches often take root, creating thickets along waterways.

The leaves are large and heart-shaped, mid-green to paler on the undersurface, glabrous, with the veins protruding prominently on the undersurface. The large yellow, crimson-throated flowers, which are 10–15 cm across, turn to a pinkish orange shade when they fall. Like all hibiscus flowers, they are produced over a long period throughout the warmer months, each flower only lasting a day or two.

The fruit is a silky-hairy capsule with five twin carpels containing hard, brown seeds.

The bark is fairly smooth and pale grey. Its fibres were used by Aboriginals for fishing nets and fishing lines. The close grained timber is almost indestructible and prized for boat building.

Outside Australia, Cottonwood occurs throughout the tropics of both hemispheres and is found in Florida, USA, where it is called Mahoe.

This is a useful tree, particularly for wet or sandy soils near the coast, which can be trained to give a dense umbrella of shade and is suited to growing beneath overhead service wires. It is easily propagated from seed.

SEASIDE MAHOE or TULIP TREE *Thespesia populnea* (L.) Sol. ex Corr. is similar in habit and habitat, being found along the tropical northern coastline of Australia, as well as in many other warm regions of the world. It features similar yellow, maroon-throated flowers and heart-shaped leaves, but differs in its fruiting capsules, which do not split open on the tree.

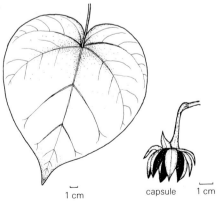

1 cm

capsule 1 cm

NATIVE FRANGIPANI

Hymenosporum flavum F. Muell.
PITTOSPORACEAE

Native Frangipani is the only Australian species of *Hymenosporum*, and is closely related to the *Pittosporum* genus, which it resembles in certain respects. It is native to the coastal brush forests of eastern Australia, extending from the Hunter River in New South Wales to Atherton in Queensland.

In tropical Queensland some trees grow to 25 m with a stem diameter of 30 cm or more, but further south it is much smaller. In cultivation it is usually only a small, very slender and upright tree up to 10 m high. Bark is grey and roughish, and the branches are sparse, radiating in whorls from the main stem. The deep lustrous green leaves, which resemble those of *Pittosporum*, are alternately grouped at the ends of the twiggy branchlets, oval-oblong in shape, and 7–15 cm long. This is a very fine flowering tree that begins to bloom in early spring, when the fragrant, open, tubular flowers are cream-coloured. They darken with age to a deep sulphur yellow before they drop. The effect of masses of cream and yellow flowers is very lovely. The flowering period extends to early summer. The 4 cm diameter flowers in terminal corymbs are sweetly scented, and about the size and shape of those of the Frangipani, from which the common name is derived. In other respects the tree bears no resemblance to the Frangipani at all.

Fruit capsules are hard and brown, containing numerous closely packed layers of brown, papery seeds which germinate freely.

Native Frangipani is a quick-growing, free-flowering small evergreen which is easily cultivated but requires copious watering, especially in the early stages. It is not particular as to soils, and grows quite successfully in the cooler temperate climates of Melbourne and Adelaide, though it resents frosty conditions. In cool climates it is not recommended as a lawn specimen, because of its habit of continuously dropping leaves, and its susceptibility to the effects of strong winds. It is best planted among other trees where it can receive their protection, and its slender growth harmonises well in group or clump planting.

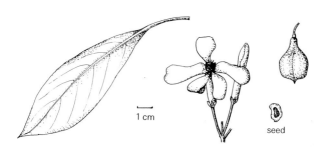

1 cm

seed

FOAM-BARK TREE, PINK FOAM BARK, FERN TREE

Jagera pseudorhus (A. Rich.) Radlk.

SAPINDACEAE

This tree is widely distributed along the coastal areas from northern Queensland to the Taree district in New South Wales but, as is the case with so many of the scrub forest species, generally only random specimens remain along country roadsides. Because of its ornamental appearance, however, it is sometimes cultivated.

This is the only species of *Jagera* occurring in Australia, although other species are found in New Guinea and the Moluccas.

Although specimens to 12 m high occur, it is usually only a small tree of 4–6 m, with dense, fern-like foliage often to near ground level, and with whitish or pale grey bark. The tree is fairly readily recognised because of its foliage and, particularly in spring, by its attractive clusters of bright orange fruits. These resemble those of the pittosporums but differ in that they are densely covered with short, stiff yellowish brown hairs.

The pinnate leaves comprise finely serrated ovate-lanceolate leaflets in 6–20 pairs, each leaflet 3–7 cm long with dense rusty hairs on the underside and stems. These leaves have a strong, somewhat unpleasant odour. The hairy egg-shaped fruiting capsules open into three valves, each containing two hard, shiny black seeds. A skin irritation can result from contact with the fine hairs on the fruits.

The rosy white flowers, individually small, occur in quite large terminal or axillary panicles, usually in September.

Apart from its ornamental value for planting in areas along the east coast of Australia, the Foam Bark Tree is a useful honey producer. Tests have shown that it is a source of saponin (soap). The bark was allegedly used during World War I to produce froth in beer making and was called the Beer Bark Tree at that time.

Aboriginals used the bark as a fish poison.

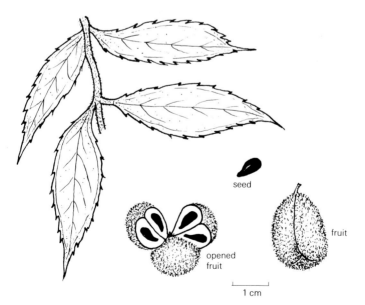

seed

opened
fruit

fruit

1 cm

BLACK GIN

Kingia australis R. Br.
XANTHORRHOEACEAE

Black Gin belongs to the same family as the better known grass trees (*Xanthorrhoea*), but is distinguished by its many drumstick-like heads of flowers, which are quite different from the solitary tall flower spikes of the grass tree.

It is found only in Western Australia, being native to the higher rainfall south-west, and growing usually in sandy, gravelly, or rocky soils. Here it is sometimes seen in groups among Karri and Jarrah trees, or as a lone sentinel on rocky outcrops in the Stirling Range and elsewhere. Wherever they occur, these magnificent and unique plants have rare beauty and great character.

The trunk is black, up to 3 m or more high, with a tufted head of rush-like leaves, the older ones reflexed or drooping. These are often crowned with a ring of flower or seed heads, like drumsticks, about 30 cm in length. The flowers are creamy white, and the seeds black.

They are long-lived and extremely slow in growth, taking many, many years to attain their characteristic appearance. It is this slowness of growth that has curtailed the planting of Black Gin in gardens, a purpose for which it is unsurpassed as a structural plant.

GRASS TREES, BLACK BOYS *Xanthorrhoea* species. These, too, are beautiful plants which are uniquely Australian. They are closely related to the Black Gin but much more common, some twelve or more species being found throughout different parts of temperate Australia. These are often stemless bushes, but some species eventually form small trees with a thick, rough stem and tufted canopy of sharp, hard, rush-like leaves. The elongated spikes of creamy white flowers bloom irregularly, and are held high above the foliage on a long, smooth stalk in spear-like fashion. These are followed by sharp, protruding seed capsules which transform the flower head into something resembling an ancient spiked club.

Grass trees are also very long-lived and slow growing. It is a tragedy to see fine mature plants being destroyed in new housing estates, where they could, if they were preserved, become unique and trouble-free assets to the garden.

Xanthorrhoea sp.

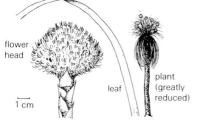

Kingia australis

flower
head

leaf

plant
(greatly
reduced)

1 cm

plant
(greatly
reduced)

Xanthorrhoea sp.

PYRAMID TREE, NORFOLK ISLAND HIBISCUS

Lagunaria patersonii G. Don

MALVACEAE

Pyramid Tree is the solitary species of the genus *Lagunaria* and belongs to the mallow family, which includes such well-known genera as *Hibiscus, Abutilon,* etc.

Native to coastal Queensland as well as to Norfolk Island, it is a very ornamental and useful tree which has long been in cultivation in Australia, as well as overseas.

The tree usually grows erect and pyramidal, with a dense, low-branching crown, and little spread. Height varies according to conditions but seldom exceeds 10–14 m. Bark is rough, dark grey, and shallowly fissured. Leaves are oval-shaped, rather rough in texture, dull green with a whitish, scurfy undersurface. The new leaves are much paler, providing a pleasing contrast.

Occurring singly in the leaf axils, the flower buds are small and conical. They open to reveal handsome, rose pink, hibiscus-like blossoms, 3–5 cm across with five velvety-textured, recurved petals. They flower over a long period during the warm months of spring, summer, and early autumn. The hard, egg-shaped fruits that follow are a pale greyish green with a rough velvety texture, and are rather like flower buds at first. They eventually turn dry at maturity, opening to reveal five valves containing the seeds. These valves are lined with a mat of fine hairs. The irritating effect these have on the skin when handled has caused the tree to be called Cow-itch Tree.

Lagunaria is successfully grown throughout Australia, particularly near the sea, where it has proved that it can withstand cold, salt-laden winds without visible 'burning off'. Tolerant of most soils including almost solid limestone, it is often used for planting on inland properties, but is not drought-resistant.

Easily raised from seed, it grows rapidly, but requires some protection from extreme cold during its early years.

seed

1 cm

RED-LEAVED PALM

Livistona mariae F. Muell.

ARECACEAE

There are several species of palms native to Australia, but the Red-leaved Palm is perhaps the most interesting, owing to its unique and isolated habitat. This tree occurs only in the Finke Gorge, popularly known as Palm Valley — a deep and beautiful, red, rocky gorge. It is situated about 150 km south-west of Alice Springs and has become one of the main tourist attractions of central Australia.

The palms grow only in deep, sandy soil in the base of the valley, often in company with River Red Gum.

The palm itself is very stately in appearance, growing very slowly to 14–20 m in height. During the earlier years the young fronds are reddish coloured, a feature which gives the tree its common name. The trunk is slender and upright, topped with a broad head of cabbage-palm leaves. These palms often rise out of fairly heavy undershrubs, giving the Palm Valley area a truly tropical appearance which contrasts strangely with the surrounding arid countryside.

The creamy flowers are borne in dense panicles, and the fruits that follow are dark brown when ripe. Seeds are the size of small marbles, and are abundantly produced, thus providing, in favourable seasons, a ready means of regeneration of this unique species.

Seen naturally against a red rocky background this stately palm is one of Australia's most interesting and beautiful trees, and is one of the rarest palms in the world.

It has been grown from seeds as far south as Adelaide, where growth is very slow, but it warrants greater attention as a garden subject, particularly in warm subtropical areas.

Livistona, which features palmate leaves and black fruits, is represented by about twenty species in Australia.

CABBAGE PALM or CABBAGE TREE PALM *L. australis*

(R. Br.) C. Martius is the most common *Livistona*, being widely distributed on the east coast from Fraser Island to Gippsland in Victoria.

The apical bud, or cabbage, of this species was regularly eaten by Aboriginals and the early settlers, whilst the leaves were used to make hats, fishing lines, nets and baskets.

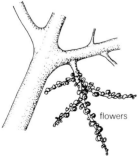
flowers

leaf stalk

1 cm

seed

fruit

BRUSH BOX, QUEENSLAND BOX

Lophostemon confertus (R. Br.) Peter G. Wilson &
J. T. Waterhouse (syn. *Tristania conferta* R. Br.)
MYRTACEAE

Well known in cultivation and a useful timber tree, Brush Box occurs naturally in the subtropical forests of New South Wales north of Newcastle and of southern Queensland, with some isolated occurrences as far north as the Atherton Tableland. It is usually an intermediate species bordering true rainforests, and prefers protected valleys and river flats with rich alluvial soils, although it is sometimes found at elevations to 1000 m. Rainfall is 750–1500 mm.

The tree is naturally tall, 40–50 m, with a straight, well-formed, shaft-like trunk, 1–2 m in diameter. Under colder, more temperate conditions, where it is frequently grown, particularly as a street tree, Brush Box is a much smaller tree, 10–15 m in height, with a symmetrical and dense conical crown; sometimes sadly abused when the tree is trained to grow beneath overhead service wires.

The bark is rough and scaly at the base but smooth on the upper trunk and branches, where the orange or dark brown colour contrasts well with the dark green shiny foliage. Juvenile leaves are soft and hairy, but mature to a glossy green with dull undersurface. Leaves are alternate, crowded into false whorls, rather large and elliptical, with a prominent midrib. Flowers are white and up to 4 cm across, with the stamens united into five feathery bundles. They appear in axillary cymes in spring. The bell-shaped fruits are three-celled and reminiscent of those of eucalypts. The ornamental timber is prized for hardwood floors and other uses.

Brush Box is a dense, ornamental evergreen which grows well in Perth and Adelaide, as well as in the eastern States. It is best suited to better-class, moist soils. Formerly known as *Tristania conferta*, Brush Box now represents the only species of *Lophostemon* in Australia, following revision of the *Tristania* group in 1982.

WATER GUM *Tristania neriifolia* (Sims) R. Br., from a restricted habitat in south-east New South Wales, is the solitary species of *Tristania*.

KANUKA or WATER GUM *Tristaniopsis laurina* (Sm.) Peter G. Wilson and J. T. Waterhouse is found over an extensive range of the east coast from Queensland to Gippsland and also occurs in New Zealand.

Both the latter species are small ornamental trees with masses of dainty yellow flowers in summer, and both favour damp situations.

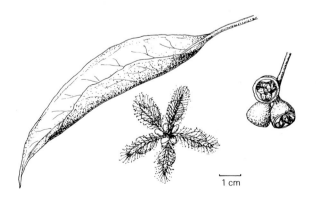

1 cm

BEAN TREE

Lysiphyllum gilvum (Bailey) Pedley
CAESALPINIACEAE

Bean Tree was formerly placed in the genus *Bauhinia* (as *B. carronii*), a large genus of plants principally found in the tropical regions of the earth. In 1977, however, a revision by Pedley separated the Australian species to include them all under *Lysiphyllum*, no *Bauhinia* species now being recorded as native to Australia, although one, *B. monandra*, has naturalised in Queensland.

Pedley lists five Australian *Lysiphyllum* species, of which *L. gilvum* is the most widely distributed. It is a tree of the arid inland areas, occurring in the Northern Territory, north-western New South Wales, many parts of Queensland and north-eastern South Australia, where it can be found on the floodplains of streams such as Cooper and Strzelecki Creeks.

Frequently seen as individual specimens, Bean Tree is conspicuous among its tree companions. A small to medium-sized tree 3–10 m high, its dense, intricate crown reaches to near ground level where the leaves and fruiting pods are eaten by stock. The tree deciduates during winter and early spring. The leaves consist of twin leaflets, each leaflet broadly ovate, 2–3 cm long by about 1·2 cm broad, with prominent longitudinal veins. The young leaves and branchlets are softly hairy but this hairyness is lost as they mature. Flowers are white or brick red, 2–3 cm across, with five open petals, the stamens long and protruding. They are arranged in short racemes of two or three and appear in spring, the flowering depending on seasonal conditions. Fruits are slightly curved flat pods, 5–10 cm long by 2–3 cm broad, containing hard, flat shining brown seeds. The timber is hard and heavy, dark brown with a fine grain. Although of quite ornamental appearance, Bean Tree is rarely cultivated and hence its reliability under cultivation is unknown.

L. carronii (F. Muell.) Pedley is a closely related tree found in the drier coastal districts of North Queensland and has been confused with *L. gilvum*. It is distinguished by its larger seed pods and the reddish brown hairs on the outside of the calyx. These are yellowish in *L. gilvum*.

seed

1 cm

QUEENSLAND NUT, POPPEL NUT

Macadamia integrifolia Maiden & Betche
PROTEACEAE

Queensland Nut is a rainforest tree of the eastern coastal scrubs from just south of Sydney to Maryborough in Queensland.

Its delicious edible nuts give it considerable economic importance. Overseas, particularly in Hawaii and California, its cultivation has become an important primary industry. In these countries improved strains have been developed from which quality thin-shelled nuts are harvested.

From seed the tree usually takes about 6–7 years to bear, but as the fruit of seedlings is unreliable, new plants should be vegetatively propagated from a good nut-bearing tree.

Under natural conditions it reaches a height of 20 m, but it seldom attains more than half this size when cultivated. The tree is very densely branched with dark green glossy leaves and a slightly rough brown bark. The leaves are very variable, 7–22 cm long, usually in whorls of three. They can be entire or divided, sometimes wavy, or harshly serrated with small, pungent teeth. New shoots are an attractive bronze or pink colour. The small creamish or pale brown flowers in long, pendulous, catkin-like racemes appear in profusion in spring, when they provide a pleasing contrast to the dark foliage.

The rounded fruits (follicles) are in clusters, and each has a soft green covering enclosing the hard-shelled brown nut. The oil-rich kernel, when toasted or salted, has a very pleasing flavour.

This is a worthwhile tree for garden culture, being ornamental as well as useful. It is slow growing in cultivation but eventually makes a permanent tree. *Macadamia* can be grown in cooler climates, but prefers rich, moist soils and copious summer watering in its early stages.

SMALL-FRUITED QUEENSLAND NUT *M. ternifolia* F. Muell. (syn. *M. minor* F. M. Bailey) is a Queensland species which is also cultivated, and requires similar growing conditions to Queensland Nut. It is of similar appearance but much smaller in stature, sometimes only shrubby.

BALL NUT *M. praealta* F. M. Bailey is also very similar and inhabits the same regions, but has a different leaf and flower arrangement, as well as larger non-edible fruits about the size of a golf ball.

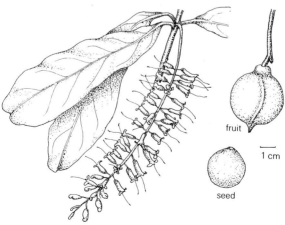

fruit

1 cm

seed

SALTWATER PAPERBARK

Melaleuca cuticularis Labill.
MYRTACEAE

Very few of the many melaleucas native to the higher rainfall
south-west of Western Australia reach tree proportions.
Saltwater Paperbark is an exception: it is one of the larger
paperbarks of these swamplands, where in certain parts it is the
dominant tree of the area. In places near Denmark it can be seen
as the only tree in waterlogged pastures where it has been
allowed to remain as shelter for stock. It is mainly found in
wet swamps from Perth to Israelite Bay, with a rare occurrence
on Kangaroo Island, SA. It is sometimes seen growing virtually
on the shoreline with its feet in salt water.

Where it still remains in natural thickets the tree is usually
spindly, crooked and small, but it is seen at its best where single
specimens remain in cleared land. Under these conditions the
tree reaches 10–12 m in height with a rather stout trunk
surmounted by a dense canopy of dark green foliage.

The main feature is its gleaming white papery bark on trunk
and branches, outstanding even in a genus noted for this feature. The narrow leaves, arranged in opposite pairs, are small,
up to 1 cm long, glabrous, and sharply pointed. The small,
white flowers which occur from June to November are in small
terminal heads of one to three, sometimes prolific. At its best,
this tree is well worthy of cultivation.

SWAMP PAPERBARK *M. rhaphiophylla* Schau. is perhaps
the largest of the western paperbarks. It inhabits sandy swamplands in the Perth district extending north as far as the
Murchison River and south to the Karri forests.

It is a small to medium-sized tree, up to 14 m high, with a
rather short, thick trunk (about 1 m in diameter), and branches
clothed in grey and white papery bark. The tree is usually
crooked or leaning with gnarled and twisted branches. More
mature specimens have a look of very great age about them.
Foliage is dark green, the leaves 1–5 cm long, very narrow, flat
or terete, and sharply pointed. The flowers are cream in terminal, rather loose spikes, and may bloom profusely in spring.

This is a useful tree for waterlogged sandy soils.

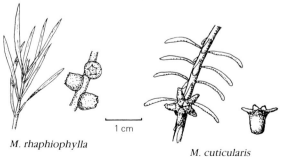

M. rhaphiophylla

1 cm

M. cuticularis

DESERT PAPERBARK, WHITE TEA-TREE

Melaleuca glomerata F. Muell.

MYRTACEAE

Desert Paperbark is a small, somewhat spreading and low branched tree up to 10 m high, inhabiting inland creeks and dry streams. It is found from the Flinders Ranges in South Australia northwards to central Australia, and in Western Australia and western New South Wales.

Paperbarks or tea-trees (the latter being more correctly the accepted common name of the leptospermums) belong to the large genus *Melaleuca*, and are also sometimes called honey myrtles, particularly the shrubby species. There are over 200 native to Australia.

The term 'paperbark' is very appropriate, particularly to the trees of the genus, many of which posséss a papery deciduous bark that hangs loosely in layers on the trunk and branches, in some species grey or creamy coloured, in others a very vivid white.

Melaleucas are distinguished botanically by the stalkless (sessile) flowers which are clustered in cylindrical spikes often like small bottlebrushes; each flower comprises very small petals but has many long stamens united into five bundles. The fruits are also sessile, small, and woody, and cluster along the branches, growing a little larger each year they remain on the plant. Each seed capsule contains numerous tiny seeds which are released after picking or fire.

Melaleucas are often the characteristic trees of swampy, poorly drained brackish soils, and are sometimes found in pure stands along the banks of streams and estuaries or lagoons where their roots are immersed in water. This is not always the case, however, as some are native to the dry regions.

Melaleuca glomerata is one such species, and is found growing in sandy soils along the dried up waterways of the inland.

It is a handsome tree, sometimes only a shrub, well suited, where conditions are favourable, to ornamental planting. Its low spreading branches afford good shade and shelter for stock. The bark is white and papery, and the leaves are grey-coloured, small, and very narrow, acutely pointed. The globular flowers, cream or yellow in colour, occur in dense terminal heads and make a fine display over the whole tree during late spring.

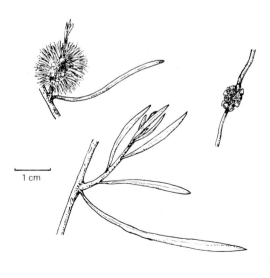

KANGAROO TEA-TREE, SOUTH AUSTRALIAN PAPERBARK

Melaleuca halmaturorum F. Muell. ex Miq.

MYRTACEAE

Kangaroo Tea-tree is a common small straggling tree of the swampy, salty soils of many parts of the South Australian coastline, especially the Coorong and the South-East, and extending into western Victoria. It is also found on Kangaroo Island and occasionally inland in South Australia around the edges of salt lagoons.

Several of the many paperbarks found in the coastal swamps of the eastern States and Western Australia are described in the following pages; but this particular species is the only papery-barked melaleuca found along the South Australian coastline. Its roots are often immersed in brackish water. Moonah (*M. lanceolata*) is also found in these parts but this is a rough-barked tree.

Kangaroo Tea-tree is a short, crooked, straggling tree up to 8 m high, sometimes forming almost grotesque shapes, resembling an enlarged specimen of Japanese bonsai. Its irregular shape is enhanced by the low-branched, crooked, but rather erect limbs and thick papery white or grey deciduous bark which hangs in loose flakes from the trunk and branches. The trunk is short and thick, buttressed at the base by horizontally spreading roots which are partly visible above the ground.

The foliage forms a rather dense canopy at the ends of the branches. The small dark green crowded leaves are glabrous, small and narrow, slightly curved, and decussate. The flowers are white and occur in terminal heads, usually in late spring.

This tree is particularly useful for planting in difficult, salty, poorly drained soils, and attempts should be made to re-establish it along the edges of streams and lakes where it was once the dominant tree. The Patawalonga River at Glenelg, an Adelaide beach suburb, is an example of an area where this tree once grew profusely and where it could be profitably re-established.

1 cm

MOONAH, BLACK TEA-TREE

Melaleuca lanceolata Otto subsp. *lanceolata*
(syn. *M. pubescens* Schau.)
MYRTACEAE

Moonah is a small tree found throughout most of temperate south-east Australia in open country in both coastal and inland situations, often on poor limy soils, but almost always in areas exceeding a 300 mm rainfall. It avoids the wetter mountainous regions.

The tree extends from the eastern edge of the Nullarbor Plain to inland southern Queensland, but is not found in Tasmania.

A bushy small tree up to about 10 m high, it is distinguished by its very dark green, almost black, foliage and rough, dark-grey bark which combine to give it quite a sombre, but characteristic appearance when not in flower. The crown is rounded, very dense and low-branched, the small twigs whitish. Leaves are small, narrow and crowded, rather thick and curved, with sharp points. The young growth is a much brighter green than the mature foliage. The flowers occur in loose fluffy cylindrical spikes at irregular periods, but the tree blooms profusely in summer, when the massed display of white blossom against the dark foliage is a very rewarding sight.

Moonah is useful as a windbreak tree for inland plantings on poor alkaline soils, or as a specimen tree for coastal or seaside situations where more favoured plants are difficult to grow. It is wind-resistant and will grow on almost any soil, and is also a good honey tree, although the quality of the honey is not first-rate.

In Western Australia, *M. lanceolata* appears in several slightly different forms which have been given subspecies status (Barlow, 1988). One of these is the Rottnest Tea-Tree (*M. lanceolata* subsp. *occidentalis*).

Another species, *M. preissiana* Schau., has been confused with *M. lanceolata* but it can easily be distinguished by its papery bark, as well as other botanical differences.

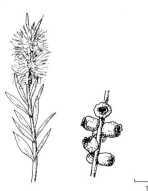

1 cm

M. preissiana

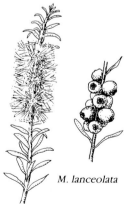
M. lanceolata

WEEPING PAPERBARK, LONG-LEAVED PAPERBARK

Melaleuca leucadendra (L.) L.

MYRTACEAE

The tree now bearing this name was the original species on which the genus *Melaleuca* was founded, having been discovered in Ambon in Indonesia, and later by Linnaeus in India. At this time the oil in the leaves was known as 'Oil of Cajuput', the tree then bearing the botanical name of *cajuput*. It is ironical that the genus was founded on a species collected outside Australia, since more than 200 species are endemic to this country, and only eight have been recorded elsewhere.

This tree belongs to a closely related group of paperbarks. These are trees of the coastal swamps and lagoons extending from just south of Sydney to the tropical north of Australia, and thence to Indonesia and Malaysia.

Weeping Paperbark is a large tree, normally no more than 20 m high, but occasionally much higher, with a thick, robust trunk supporting layers of very white papery bark which is smooth and slippery to the touch. The smaller branches and leaves hang downwards more or less vertically, giving the tree an ornamental, weeping appearance, and its common name.

The leaves are a thin, fresh green, lanceolate, up to 20 cm long by 1–3 cm wide, with five longitudinal veins. The loose, cream, bottlebrush-type flowers are fragrant and laden with nectar, much sought after by birds, bees and flying foxes. Flowering occurs mainly from winter to spring. The bark is used for lining hanging baskets and the oil in the leaves has medicinal value.

Melaleuca leucadendra is native to Papua New Guinea and Indonesia, as well as northern Australia, where it extends across the continent from Western Australia to Queensland. It is very common along the coastal districts of northern Queensland, favouring moist, sandy soils and sometimes growing virtually on the beach. It is a feature of some of the beach townships north of Cairns, where clusters of large trees of great beauty have been retained in places and give character to the streetscape.

A closely related northern paperbark, *M. argentea* W. V. Fitzgerald, is usually a smaller tree with narrower leaves that are silvery, particularly on the new growth. It inhabits river banks of the 'Top End', from the Kimberleys to north Queensland.

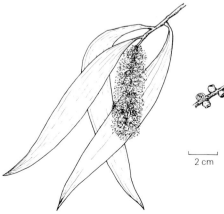

2 cm

NARROW-LEAF PAPERBARK

Melaleuca linariifolia Smith
MYRTACEAE

One of the many paperbarks found along the coastal estuaries and streams from southern New South Wales to Cape Melville in Queensland, this particular species occurs from about Jervis Bay in the south to Gladstone in Queensland. It is a very beautiful tree, 7–14 m high, with a white papery bark and rather thick trunk buttressed with horizontally spreading roots visible slightly above ground level. The crown is usually bushy with bright green, or bluish green, soft foliage. The leaves are 3 cm or more long and narrow, arranged in opposite pairs on the branches.

Flowering is prolific, so that the whole tree appears to be covered with snow. The fluffy white flowers occur in loose bundles held prominently above the foliage, the new growth continuing during the flowering period. The main flowering is in November.

A valuable ornamental and street tree in reasonably wet districts, it prefers non-alkaline soils and is sometimes difficult to establish.

M. linariifolia var. *trichostachya* (Lindl.) Benth. is similar and closely related. It is of wide distribution, extending from the north-east coast across the Great Dividing Range to many parts of inland Queensland and the Northern Territory where it follows dry sandy streams, but retains a constant character throughout. *M. alternifolia* Cheel is a smaller but closely related tree with narrower, but alternate leaves. It has a more restricted range, being found mainly between the Stroud and Richmond Rivers in New South Wales. The leaves of both species are rich in oils.

PRICKLY-LEAF PAPERBARK *M. styphelioides* Smith is another beautiful paperbark of the coastal division of New South Wales and southern Queensland. Although different botanically, it is mentioned because it is commonly cultivated. It frequently reaches 20 m in height with small, broad, prickly leaves and masses of small cream flower spikes in late spring. This useful tree grows on most soils, including those which are poorly drained and brackish.

The timber of all species is very durable in damp ground or wet conditions.

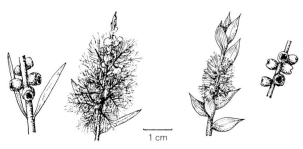

M. linariifolia   *M. styphelioides*

1 cm

BROAD-LEAVED PAPERBARK, FIVE-VEINED PAPERBARK

Melaleuca quinquenervia (Cav.) S. T. Blake
MYRTACEAE

This is one of the most common large paperbark trees of the streams, swamps and estuaries of the east coast of Australia, particularly in northern New South Wales and southern Queensland, where pure stands can be encountered.

Although it extends from near Sydney to Cape York, usually within 40 km of the coast, it is more common in the southern half of its range, *M. leucadendra* (p. 258) being more prevalent in the north. The tree extends to southern New Guinea, Indonesia and New Caledonia. It favours flat, moist land usually with sandy topsoil, where pure stands are often encountered.

Broad-leaved Paperbark is an erect tree to 25 m high, but normally only 8–12 m. Bark is greyish white, thick and papery and useful for hanging baskets. The leaves are stiff and leathery, 4–10 cm long by 1·5–3 cm broad with five longitudinal nerves, lanceolate-elliptic to oblanceolate in shape. The oil from the leaves could have commercial value, but is rarely extracted.

The flower spikes are dense, of the bottlebrush type, 2–5 cm long, and cream, white, or occasionally reddish in colour. These are borne in autumn–winter. The small woody seed capsules are about 5 mm in diameter.

At its best this is an ornamental tree, and one of the few suited to water-logged conditions exposed to strong winds. Its timber is durable in water and is useful for house stumps and fence posts.

M. viridiflora Sol. ex Gaert., also known as Broad-leaved Paperbark, is a related species which extends from north of Maryborough in Queensland, across the Northern Territory to the Kimberleys in Western Australia. It is distinguished by its usually smaller, often shrubby, stature, its larger and coarser, broadly elliptic leaves, and its larger, showy flowers. The latter appear in winter and are normally yellowish green, but sometimes a vivid red. This is a variable species with several named subspecies.

1 cm

stamens

WHITE CEDAR, BEAD TREE

Melia azedarach L. var. *australasica* C. DC.
MELIACEAE

One of the few Australian deciduous trees, White Cedar inhabits the brush forests of the east coast, extending from the Illawarra district in New South Wales north to the coastal brush forests of Queensland. It is also native to India, Indonesia, and New Guinea.

The tree grows naturally very tall and long-stemmed in its forest environment, but when cultivated has a much shorter and more spreading appearance, seldom exceeding 10–15 m in height.

Once frequently planted as a park, garden, or street tree, it has since been found to have a root system unsuitable for footpaths. This and the untidy dropping of the ripe fruits have caused it to fall from favour. Often, existing trees have been mutilated by constant and severe pruning. Left untouched, however, this can be a very lovely tree with an appealing wide, almost horizontal, branching habit, providing good shade in summer. Being deciduous, it does not block the sunlight in winter.

The foliage is a handsome bright glossy green, the alternate, compound leaves usually bipinnate, with numerous leaflets. Individual leaflets are ovate and prominently toothed on the margins. The lilac flowers are fragrant and appear in erect terminal panicles that are prolific in spring. The fruits, which are in clusters, are oval to round, bead-like drupes with a hard bony stone. They are initially pale green in colour, but ripen to a yellowish brown, and remain on the tree long after the leaves have fallen. Bark is grey and slightly furrowed, and the timber light, open-grained, and useful for interior woodwork.

Despite its subtropical habitat, White Cedar is an extremely adaptable tree that can be easily grown in most soils and situations in a rainfall as low as 300–400 mm.

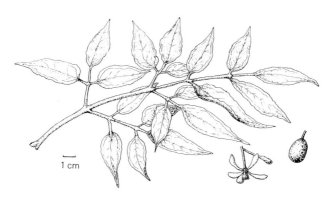

1 cm

SUGARWOOD

Myoporum platycarpum R. Br.
MYOPORACEAE

Sugarwood is a widespread tree found growing in the drier parts of temperate Australia, often in poor, limy soils. It is seldom seen in colonies, but is usually scattered over large areas as isolated specimens or in small groups, particularly in open, flat country.

The genus *Myoporum* consists of about thirty species, half of them Australian. They vary from prostrate ground cover plants to small trees up to about 10 m high.

The name Sugarwood was given to this particular species because of the sweet resin which it sometimes exudes. This resin was used by the Aboriginals as an adhesive cement.

When young, the trees are quite tidy and symmetrical, although they are usually seen as sturdy old specimens of great character with many gnarled and dead limbs, but with upright trunks covered with very rough, dark, flaky bark. On drooping branchlets, the leaves, about 5 cm long, are a pale, shiny green, narrow but fleshy, with a few small teeth on the upper part. They contrast well with the dark bark. The small starry, white or pinkish flowers are abundantly produced in dense clusters from August to December. Fruits are small, rather fleshy drupes, each of which contains two seeds.

The soft yellow timber is fragrantly scented. For this reason the tree is sometimes wrongly called Sandalwood.

This is a useful fodder tree and an important species in dry inland situations. It is a protected plant in South Australia.

BOOBIALLA *M. insulare* R. Br. is a much-used species, native to all States except Queensland and the Northern Territory. A densely foliaged evergreen growing up to 10 m or sometimes a shrub, it resists wind and fire very well and is often used for dense shelter belts around farm houses. This species is also useful for coastal planting as it withstands salt winds very well.

The rather large, somewhat fleshy leaves are a bright shiny green, and the starry white flowers are followed by fleshy purplish fruits or berries. It flowers for most of the year.

All the myoporums are easily grown in most soils.

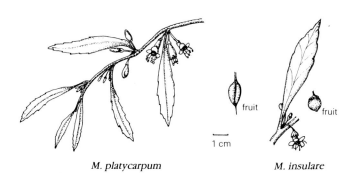

M. platycarpum   *M. insulare*

fruit   fruit

1 cm

ANTARCTIC BEECH, TASMANIAN MYRTLE

Nothofagus cunninghamii (Hook.) Oersted
FAGACEAE

The genus *Nothofagus*, in Australia, has four species. It is the · Southern Hemisphere representative of the European beech trees (*Fagus*), which are deciduous but otherwise very similar in general appearance.

Antarctic Beech is a large, often spreading, evergreen tree, found in moist, rich mountain valleys of parts of Victoria and Tasmania. Once commonly encountered in the Otway Ranges, Baw Baw Mountains, and Upper Yarra districts in Victoria, it has been so often destroyed by fire and by human activity that it is now quite rare in these areas. It is common in Tasmania, where it is known as Tasmanian Myrtle.

At its robust best, the tree reaches heights exceeding 33 m, with a trunk large in girth, and covered with thick, rough bark. It is often seen with more than one main stem joined at the base, a feature which sometimes adds to its characteristically handsome appearance under natural conditions.

The foliage is deep green and dense, the leaves being roundish in shape, 6–12 mm long, with rather wavy, toothed margins, and arranged in fan-like sprays. In early spring the young foliage is a rich bronze colour, and strikingly beautiful. Flowers, appearing in early summer, are small and catkin-like; the male flowers are produced low down on the stem; the female flowers occur in threes on the upper part. Fruits are also usually in threes, and contain winged seeds which are seldom viable after about 12 months. Regeneration from seed is very slow.

Timber is soft and reddish-coloured, polishes and dresses well, and has been used in joinery work.

NEGROHEAD BEECH *N. moorei* (F. Muell.) Krasser, sometimes also called Antarctic Beech, is a closely related large tree native to the high altitudes of the Macpherson Range in Queensland, and the mountain slopes of coastal New South Wales. This lovely tree is readily distinguished by its similarly shaped but larger leaves which are 4–5 cm long.

TANGLEFOOT *N. gunnii* (Hook.) Oersted is a truly deciduous species from alpine Tasmania. It is a straggly shrub or small tree whose leaves turn bright yellow in the autumn.

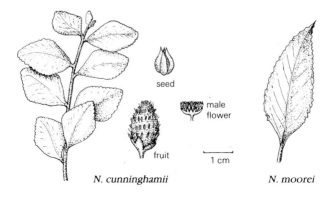

N. cunninghamii

seed

fruit

male
flower

1 cm

N. moorei

WESTERN AUSTRALIAN CHRISTMAS TREE

Nuytsia floribunda (Labill.) R. Br. ex Fenzl
LORANTHACEAE

Native only to Western Australia, Christmas Tree is one of Australia's most remarkable trees, and indeed, would rank as one of the finest flowering trees on earth.

It is a member of the well-known mistletoe family which consists mostly of semiparasitic shrubs growing on the branches of host trees. Christmas Tree differs in that it forms a tree with roots in the soil which depend partly on the roots of other plants for their nourishment.

The tree has quite an extensive habitat range from the Murchison River in the north to Israelite Bay on the south coast, and extending in places some 300 km inland. Rainfall is in the 350–1100 mm range, and soils are always sandy, peaty, or of granite origin.

It is not a graceful tree, often possessing a very thick rough-barked trunk, stiff upright branches, and rather heavy looking foliage. The timber is very soft and weak, and the tree is unsafe to climb even for children. Leaves are narrow, pointed, and of thick texture.

Christmas Tree begins to flower in October but reaches its full brilliance around Christmas time. Flowers are so abundant at this time that the whole tree becomes a glowing mass of golden orange. This tree in full bloom against a blue summer sky is a never-to-be-forgotten sight.

Nuytsia is remarkable in that the seeds germinate to produce 3–6 cotyledons (seed leaves) instead of the normal two.

This is an exceptional tree which fortunately seems destined to remain in the Western Australian landscape for many years to come. Farmers have recognised that it is unique and worth preserving, and it can be seen left in paddocks (completely denuded of other tree cover), apparently feeding off the roots of grasses. It cannot be destroyed by fire and recovers by vigorous suckering, blooming even better than before.

Many attempts have been made by enthusiasts to grow this tree, but there is little evidence to date that it can be cultivated successfully.

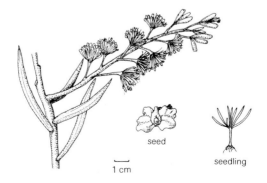

seed

seedling

1 cm

BLEEDING HEART, QUEENSLAND POPLAR TREE

Omalanthus populifolius Grah.
EUPHORBIACEAE

This is a widely distributed small tree which is usually found on the fringes of rainforest, extending from East Gippsland in Victoria to the Daintree River, or beyond, in north Queensland. It is also native to Papua New Guinea, Lord Howe and Norfolk Islands and Malesia. However, it is better known as a cultivated garden tree of small proportions and rapid growth. It often appears in home gardens as self-sown specimens, the seeds being readily spread by birds.

The tree rarely exceeds 5 m high, although occasional larger specimens can be found in the wild. The shape is normally wide-branching but pyramidal. Its attraction lies in its soft heart-shaped or rhomboid leaves, the old leaves turning bright red and some of these usually being present at all times among the light green younger leaves. It is this feature from which the common name is derived. The alternate leaves vary in size from up to 20 cm long by 15 cm wide (at the younger stage) to only 3 cm long by nearly this width, and have long, thin red stalks.

The flowers are not significant, each flower being very tiny and yellowish in colour; they are borne in narrow terminal spikes about 5–7 cm long. These appear in spring to summer and at other times, depending on seasons. Fruit is almost black, a two-lobed, thin-stalked capsule with two cells, a seed usually being present in each cell. The black seeds are enveloped in a yellowish aril.

Bleeding Heart is an easily grown, trouble-free, small tree with ornamental foliage, which can be successfully grown in all Australian States and capital cities. It is not fussy about soils. It also makes an attractive pot plant, but, because of its rapid growth, is not really suited to pot culture.

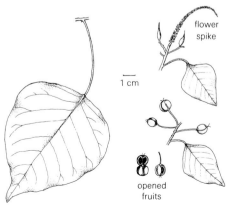

flower spike

1 cm

opened fruits

PINK SILKY OAK, SATIN OAK

Oreocallis wickhamii (W. Hill & F. Muell.)
W. Hill & F. Muell. ex Sleumer
PROTEACEAE

There are two species of *Oreocallis* in Australia, both producing conspicuous heads of bright red waratah-like flowers in abundance which can make a magnificent display during spring months; yet neither species is particularly well known nor popular for garden culture. Unfortunately, the photograph does not do justice to the floral beauty of this tree. It is the floral emblem of Eacham Shire in north Queensland.

The genus, which is closely related to the waratahs (*Telopea*), extends into New Guinea and is also found in South America. In Australia they are trees of subtropical to tropical rainforest, *O. wickhamii* being native only to the Cairns district north to Daintree, and including the eastern slopes of the tablelands. Although the tree has sometimes been called Tree Waratah it differs from *Telopea* in that its inflorescences are not in dense clusters (capitate), but are shortly raceme-like, and they lack a conspicuous involucre — a whorl of bracts beneath the inflorescence. Birds are attracted to the flowers.

In its native rainforest habitat Pink Silky Oak grows erect to 25 m high with a trunk diameter up to 60 cm, but, like so many other rainforest trees, it is much smaller in cultivation, where 10 m appears to be about its maximum height. Bark is rough and grey, and the leaves are smooth, a deep lustrous green, and generally entire but variable, being deeply lobed in the juvenile stages and sometimes for some years thereafter. They are up to 20 cm long and form an attractive frame for the red flowers. The fruit is a woody capsule, almost cylindrical, or elliptical, with a long beak; it contains several winged brown seeds. Timber is soft and durable, pinkish in colour, and valuable commercially.

In cultivation, Pink Silky Oak favours heavy soils with assured moisture and, to the author's knowledge, it has not been successfully grown south of Sydney. It is an ideal tree for Brisbane gardens, where it can be grown in full sun or shade.

The other Australian species, *O. pinnata* (Maid. & Betche) Sleumer, is sometimes known as QUEENSLAND WARATAH TREE but, unlike *O. wickhamii*, is more common in northern New South Wales. It extends from Dorrigo to the Macpherson Range in southern Queensland. It is a similar tree with either entire or pinnate leaves, hence its specific name.

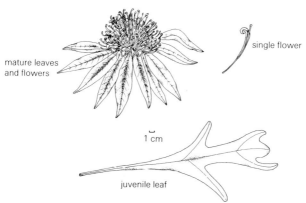

mature leaves
and flowers

single flower

1 cm

juvenile leaf

SOUR PLUM, EMU APPLE BUSH

Owenia acidula F. Muell.
MELIACEAE

This small, attractive tree of the inland is noted for its plum-like fruits which were freely eaten by the Aboriginals. It is found in South Australia on the flood plain of Cooper Creek, but is a more common tree in Queensland, New South Wales and the Northern Territory, particularly the arid to semiarid areas extending into the subhumid zones. The tree is usually found singly or in small stands, occurring on a variety of soil types, but is rarely plentiful.

Sour Plum is a densely crowned, neat-growing tree, usually 5–8 m high, with shining, drooping foliage which is often pruned regularly from ground level by stock.

The compound leaves are usually 12–16 cm long, comprising oblique pairs of linear-lanceolate leaflets, each leaflet 2–4 cm long by 4–9 mm broad. The young shoots are sticky. The foliage somewhat resembles that of the Peppercorn Tree (*Schinus molle*), but is a much darker green.

Occurring in short axillary panicles, the small five-petalled whitish flowers are not conspicuous. They are produced in spring. Fruits are globular, dark purplish red spotted drupes, 2–3 cm in diameter, hanging downwards on pendulous stalks. They have a sharp, acidic taste.

The bark is rough, a dark grey in colour, and the timber is red, with a milky sap. Although Sour Plum is an ornamental tree, especially suited to dry areas where it could be used advantageously as a small shade tree, little is known of it in cultivation. This is no doubt due to the difficulty of propagating the species from seed, and further research is required to bring this handsome Australian tree into cultivation. It suckers freely from the roots and this could be a means of propagation.

There are five other Australian species of *Owenia*, none of them well known.

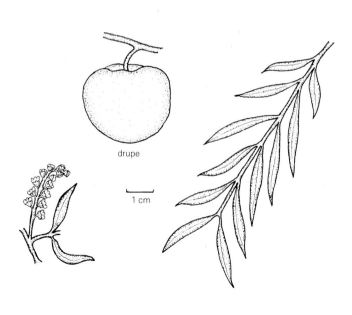

drupe

1 cm

SCREW PINE, SCREW PALM

Pandanus spiralis R. Br.

PANDANACEAE

Pandanus is a genus of plants from tropical and subtropical areas of the world. In Australia there are approximately twelve species, all of which are found in the northern half of the continent. The screw pines in Australia are not well known, and studies of native species are still being made.

Pandanus spiralis is one of the most widespread in Australia and extends from the Kimberley district in Western Australia, across the Northern Territory to Cape York Peninsula. It favours swampy localities which are usually flooded during the 'wet' season, and is often found along the edges of streams and lagoons. A waterlily lagoon with a background grouping of screw pines is a wonderful sight.

The trees grow to about 5–7 m in height. Each branch is topped with a group of long, narrow leaves, 1–2 m long, arranged in spiral fashion. The edges of the leaves are armed with sharp teeth or spines. Flowers are small and produced in dense clusters which eventually develop into large pineapple-like fruits, sometimes reddish in colour. When ripe these break up into segments, which release the seed and fall to the ground.

Many *Pandanus* species have prop-like roots which grow from the main trunk into the ground forming extra supports. *P. spiralis*, however, has no such supports and is easily distinguished by their absence.

Fibre from the leaves has been used for sack-making, while Aboriginals have used parts of the fruit for food.

Other screw pines in Australia include *P. aquaticus* F. Muell., which is found along watercourses; *P. basedowii* C. H. Wright, which inhabits rocky cliffs in Arnhem Land; and *P. pedunculatus* R. Br. which is an east coast species from Queensland and New South Wales, where it can be seen growing almost to the water's edge at beaches.

Pandanus pedunculatus

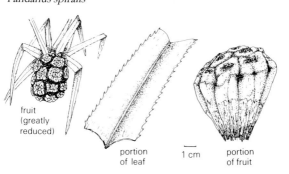

Pandanus spiralis

fruit
(greatly
reduced)

portion
of leaf

1 cm

portion
of fruit

YELLOW FLAME TREE

Peltophorum pterocarpum (DC.) Backer ex K. Heyne
CAESALPINIACEAE

This lovely flowering deciduous tree is a native of the tropics and drier monsoonal regions. It is the only species of *Peltophorum* in Australia, where it is found in the Darwin area, Arnhem Land, and north and central Queensland. The tree is also a native of New Guinea, Malaysia, the Philippines, South-East Asia and India.

Yellow Flame Tree can reach about 18 m but is usually much lower and spreading in cultivation. It is grown in Brisbane as a street tree and in Darwin as a street or park specimen tree, ideal for shade. The bark is light grey and the young branches and inflorescences are covered with soft, silky brown hairs.

The bipinnate leaves are large, 15–40 cm long, divided into pinnae 6–12 cm long, with individual leaflets 1–2 cm long. These are dark green and shiny above, but paler and with soft brownish hairs on the underside.

The flowers occur in spectacular terminal heads, clustered to form panicles, 30–45 cm long, each individual flower being bright yellow and 3–4 cm across, with five shaggy or crinkled petals. Buds are brown and softly hairy, contrasting well with the opened flowers. Flowering occurs at the end of the 'dry' season, about October, when the trees are very conspicuous.

Appearing with the flowers are the fruiting pods, reddish brown in colour, 8–10 cm long by 2–2·5 cm across with winged margins. The pods contain 1–5 flattish yellow-brown seeds which germinate freely if softened in boiling water, although they may take a month or more to do so.

A yellow-brown dye obtained from the bark is used in the batik industry in Asia.

Yellow Flame Tree is a fine shade or street tree for the warm subtropical to tropical areas of Australia, where it can be grown in a range of soils where moisture is assured and frosts are not severe.

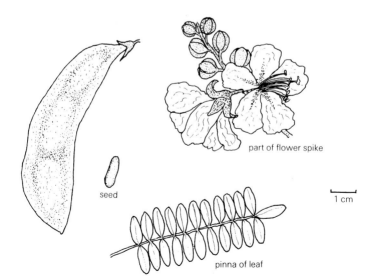

seed

part of flower spike

1 cm

pinna of leaf

NATIVE APRICOT, BERRIGAN

Pittosporum phylliraeoides DC.
PITTOSPORACEAE

Native Apricot is a dry area species of an otherwise subtropical to tropical genus in Australia. *Pittosporum* is a large genus of evergreen plants, well represented in both Australia and New Zealand, and belonging to the family Pittosporaceae, of which all other genera are entirely Australian. The name is derived from the sticky pulp surrounding the seeds.

Native Apricot is found in areas of extremely low to moderate rainfall throughout temperate Australia. On the fringe of the vast Nullarbor Plain tree life gradually gives way to bluebush and grasses, but among this vegetation Native Apricot can be seen persisting as isolated stunted specimens for many kilo-metres, it and Miljee (*Acacia oswaldii*) being the last remaining plants of any height in this very arid terrain.

In the better parts of its range it grows into a very handsome, graceful tree, 7–14 m high. It is easily recognised by its long, very slender, but sparse, weeping branches which often droop to near ground level, its bright green foliage, and its pale grey, smoothish trunk. These conspicuous features are unmistakable when it is seen among its dry area companions.

The bright green, glabrous leaves are 5–10 cm long by about 6–10 mm wide, with a small, hooked point. Flowers are small and bell-shaped, pale yellow in colour, and borne in masses in summer. These are followed by attractive small orange fruits shaped like small apricots which split open when ripe to reveal deep red sticky seeds. A tree laden with these colourful fruits is a lovely sight during autumn and winter.

This tree is easily cultivated, particularly in light soils, and tolerates much wetter conditions than it usually encounters in its natural environment. It is particularly ornamental as a weeping specimen tree, and should receive more favourable consideration than it does, as a garden subject.

Native Apricot is protected by law in South Australia.

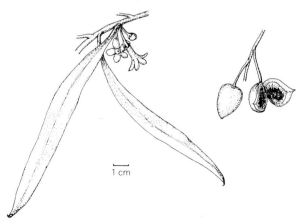

1 cm

QUEENSLAND PITTOSPORUM

Pittosporum rhombifolium A. Cunn. ex Hook.
PITTOSPORACEAE

This small, but very ornamental, tree is not often grown, which is a pity because it displays masses of very showy fruits during autumn and through winter when colour is lacking in gardens in the southern parts of Australia.

It occurs naturally along the east coast subtropical regions from the Clarence River district in northern New South Wales to Proserpine in Queensland.

Queensland Pittosporum rarely grows larger than 10–12 m high, with an upright but well-foliaged habit. In cultivation it may only grow into a bushy shrub. The aromatic, alternate leaves are a glossy green, broad and rhomboid with wavy, or bluntly toothed, margins.

In late summer in Adelaide (in September in Queensland), masses of small, creamy, sweetly scented flowers appear in terminal clusters. These are followed by the handsome apricot or orange berries mentioned above, about 1 cm in diameter, and roughly globular or pear-shaped. The fruits set against the handsome foliage are the feature of the tree, particularly as they are displayed conspicuously over a long period. Seeds, usually two per fruit, are black and shiny. Bark is grey and slightly rough.

This tree is sometimes grown as a street tree in northern New South Wales and Queensland. It prefers non-limy, moist soils and a fairly protected situation, as its root system is shallow.

BRISBANE LAUREL *P. revolutum* Ait. is a dense, compact and attractive small tree or shrub, found from Gippsland in Victoria to southern Queensland.

Leaves are light green, 5–10 cm broad, lanceolate, and covered with rust-coloured hairs on the undersurface. The small, attractive yellow flowers are followed by egg-shaped fruits up to 2·5 cm long containing red, sticky seeds.

This species favours similar growing conditions to *P. rhombifolium* and is well worth cultivating.

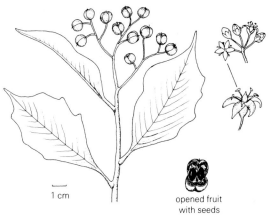

1 cm

opened fruit
with seeds

SWEET PITTOSPORUM, MOCK ORANGE

Pittosporum undulatum Vent.
PITTOSPORACEAE

A commonly cultivated tree, Sweet Pittosporum is an inhabitant of the subtropical to temperate forests of the east coast extending south from Brisbane to north-east Victoria, with a rare outlier in north-west Tasmania. Except for *P. phylliraeoides* (see p. 282), all species of the genus in Australia are found in the high-rainfall subtropical to tropical areas, usually growing dense and bushy, under 14 m in height.

Sweet Pittosporum is a dense, bushy-crowned tree up to 10 m high, often with foliage to near ground level and grey bark rather like coarse sandpaper. The laurel-like leaves are dark glossy green, paler underneath, with wavy margins, and occur in whorls at the ends of the twigs. The tree flowers in September when the terminal bunches of pale cream, bell-shaped flowers spread their strong fragrance into the surrounding areas. The 12 mm diameter fruits which follow are in handsome clusters, a bright orange in colour, and open to reveal sticky red insides and black seeds.

This tree is easily grown where rainfall is moderate, and has been extensively cultivated in such places as Adelaide where it has regenerated naturally in certain Hills districts. It can be grown under large established trees, and is useful for this reason as well as being a good ornamental evergreen shade or specimen tree. If properly planted it can also make a useful clipped hedge. The tree's main drawback is its susceptibility to scale insects which sometimes spoil the handsome deep green foliage.

Although there is a form of this species in cultivation with cream margins to the leaves, the commonly grown variegated pittosporum originates from the New Zealand species *P. eugenoides*. Several other New Zealand species are also cultivated in Australia.

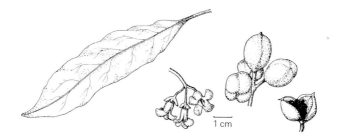

1 cm

BROWN PINE, SHE PINE, ILLAWARRA PLUM

Podocarpus elatus R. Br. ex Endl.

PODOCARPACEAE

Brown Pine is a fairly large conifer of the coastal scrub forests which extend from the Illawarra district of New South Wales northwards to Cairns in Queensland. Mature trees reach 45 m or more under these conditions, and are a conspicuous feature of the predominantly dark green jungle with their very pale green, soft new foliage.

A genus which is widespread throughout the Southern Hemisphere (there are six Australian species), *Podocarpus* differs from most other conifers by its absence of woody, seed-bearing cones, the seeds instead being borne on fleshy scales.

Younger specimens of Brown Pine often form a compact, broadly conical evergreen tree with shiny green foliage to the ground. The trunk is seldom buttressed but often irregularly indented or fluted. The dark brown bark is thin and finely fissured. The sharply pointed leaves are narrow and long, alternate, and on very short stalks with a glossy upper surface. Male and female 'flower' spikes are small, and on separate trees, appearing in spring.

The female trees produce fruits consisting of a fleshy plum-shaped receptacle of a purplish colour, about 2·5 cm in diameter. These are edible and can be made into a tasty jelly. They bear a seed at their apex similar to that of the Native Cherry (*Exocarpos*).

The tough, durable timber is golden brown, silky-textured, and particularly attractive for featured woodwork.

This is a fine, ornamental tree, best suited to rich, moist, non-alkaline soils. It requires some protection.

BLACK PINE *P. amarus* Blume is a similar tree with dark bark, native to the Atherton Tableland district of northern Queensland, and extending to New Guinea and nearby islands. The receptacles on the fruits are not as developed as those of Brown Pine, but the seeds are red and twice the size.

MOUNTAIN BROWN PINE *P. lawrencei* Hook. f. is a small, gnarled, broad-leaved conifer from alpine regions (altitudes exceeding 1000 m) of Victoria, New South Wales, and Tasmania. It bears succulent red fruits.

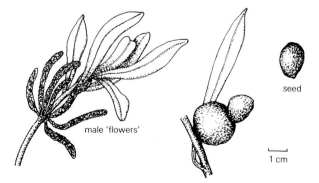

male 'flowers'

seed

1 cm

DEEP YELLOW-WOOD, TULIP SATINWOOD

Rhodosphaera rhodanthema Engl.
ANACARDIACEAE

Deep Yellow-wood is a tropical rainforest tree of the coastal areas of New South Wales north of the Clarence River, and Queensland, where it extends some 160 km inland.

Compared with many of the trees found in these luxuriant forests, this is only a small tree usually under 16 m in height, although it sometimes grows taller. In cultivation it is a shapely, rather wide-spreading tree up to 10 m high with handsome pinnate foliage; it makes an ideal garden shade and specimen tree for a well-watered lawn.

The bark of the tree is rough, grey or brown in colour, and very scaly. When cut it is a bright red or pink and exudes a sticky white gum.

The leaves are alternate and pinnate, being made up of 4–13 leaflets arranged in opposite pairs, each leaflet 5–7 cm long. The young shoots are very downy, being covered with rust-coloured hairs which sometimes persist to the underside of the mature leaves and give the foliage a brownish tinge. The branches are spotted with small raised dots (lenticels).

The small flowers, which are bright red with yellow anthers, are borne in large terminal panicles in spring, when they make a showy display. These are followed by masses of attractive, grape-like bunches of berry-like fruits which ripen to a shining reddish brown colour. Each fruit is about 12 mm in diameter. When dried they are excellent subjects for floral art arrangement.

When first cut, the heartwood is a bright yellow. This gives the tree its common name. The timber is sometimes used for fancy woodwork and polishes to an attractive pale yellow colour.

Deep Yellow-wood is an ornamental tree which grows to a good shape and size for average suburban gardens. Unfortunately it is not well known and has not received much attention as a cultivated tree. It requires plenty of water and prefers rich soils, but is adaptable, and grows well as far south as Adelaide.

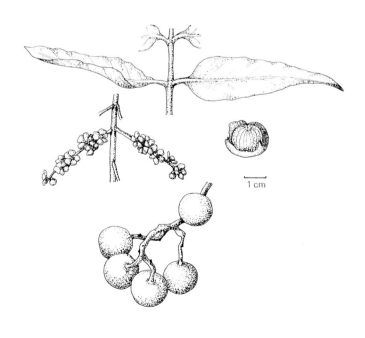

QUANDONG, NATIVE PEACH

Santalum acuminatum (R. Br.) A. DC.

SANTALACEAE

Although well known by name, Quandong has become quite rare in many places where it once grew freely. In South Australia, in particular, both Quandong and Bitter Quandong are protected plants, although it is doubtful if this law is respected by many citizens. It is an inhabitant of low to moderate rainfall and light soil areas of temperate Australia, and is still commonly encountered in Western Australia. Quandong belongs to the sandalwood family, all members of which are root parasites, being nourished by sucker-like attachments on the roots of host plants. They are related to the mistletoes, which are also parasites (see *Nuytsia*, p. 270).

Quandong is only a small compact tree, often a shrub, with long, lanceolate, rather fleshy pale grey-green leaves on slender branchlets. The small white flowers in terminal panicles are insignificant, but are followed, usually in summer, by attractive, succulent, rounded red fruits on long pendulous stalks. These fruits are edible and, although rather sour when eaten fresh, can be made into excellent jam and preserves. They contain a round, light brown, roughly pitted stone (endocarp), often used for children's playthings. The kernel is edible and very oily, with a burning taste; emus love it, and play an important part in spreading the seed. The timber is also oily and was used by the Aboriginals for creating fire by friction.

Quandongs are grown commercially on a small property near Quorn, South Australia.

BITTER QUANDONG *S. murrayanum* (T. L. Mitchell) C. A. Gardn. is a very similar tree with drooping foliage from the same areas, but distinguished by its smaller flowers which appear in axillary panicles, by its brownish, bitter fruits, and by the stone, which in this case is only slightly pitted.

FRAGRANT SANDALWOOD *S. spicatum* (R. Br.) A. DC. is a crooked, rough-barked tree growing to 8 m found in the Flinders Ranges and northern South Australia, and commonly in southern Western Australia. The tiny flowers in axillary panicles are fragrant, as is the wood, which has been exported for use as incense in Chinese temples. It is an excellent fuel and is used for firing brick kilns.

PLUM BUSH *S. lanceolatum* R. Br. from inland Australia sometimes reaches tree proportions. It has glaucous leaves, small purple fruits, and aromatic wood.

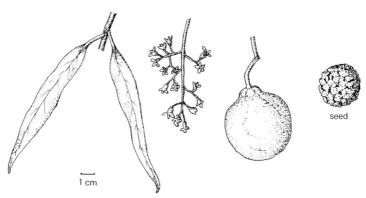

seed

1 cm

UMBRELLA TREE

Schefflera actinophylla Harms.
(syn. *Brassaia actinophylla* Endl.)
ARALIACEAE

Umbrella Tree comes from the rainforests of northern Queensland, where it grows 14–16 m tall, sometimes beginning its life as an epiphyte in the branches of a host tree.

The tree is very adaptable, and is extensively cultivated, seldom growing much larger than about 8 m high, particularly in the cooler more temperate areas, where it can be grown easily.

In cultivation it usually forms several slender main stems arising from the rootstock. The large palmate leaves are attached by very long stalks (40–70 cm long) which are arranged alternately around these main stems. Each leaf comprises (usually 12–15) large leathery leaflets of a deep lustrous green on individual stalks several centimetres long. These are attached to the end of the main stalk in a circular umbrella-like formation. The younger leaves appearing at the top of each stem are a much paler, shining green.

The attractive bright red flowers occur on long upright spikes. Their arrangement resembles the tentacles of an octopus, and in Hawaii the tree is known as Octopus Tree. The flowers change to black as the seed pods develop. Away from its native warm climate Umbrella Tree does not flower regularly, although in some years it is quite free-flowering, depending on seasonal conditions.

Not fussy as regards soils, Umbrella Tree is easily grown if given plenty of water and a sunny position. Areas where frosts are severe should be avoided. It is a tree requiring very little attention, seldom producing any vigorous unwanted branches requiring pruning, and causing no problems with leaf drop.

This tree has many uses and is a fine structural plant for producing a tropical effect in the garden. In the more tropical parts of Queensland and New South Wales it is successfully grown as a street tree.

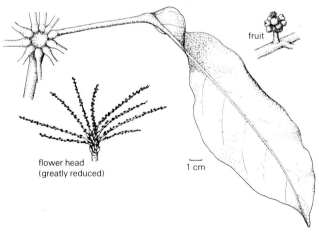

flower head
(greatly reduced)

fruit

1 cm

WHEEL OF FIRE, FIREWHEEL TREE

Stenocarpus sinuatus Endl.
PROTEACEAE

Wheel of Fire Tree is an upright, non-spreading tree, well known in cultivation, where it grows quite successfully in much cooler climates than its native habitat. It is a tropical rainforest species of the east coast, extending from northern New South Wales to the Atherton Tableland in Queensland; it often grows in dense jungle where it reaches 14–35 m in height.

The tree has a slender grey or dark brown trunk with wrinkled bark. It is densely clothed with rich green, glossy foliage and soft, downy, bronze-coloured new growth. The large leaves are extremely variable, and of firm texture. Some are entire, usually with wavy margins, others slightly divided, or deeply lobed.

It is the curiously shaped flowers that are the conspicuous feature of this tree. They are borne in large, prominent clusters during autumn and early winter, when they make a spectacular display. The flowers are 4–7 cm long and arranged in a circular fashion like the spokes of a wheel. Each flower (or spoke) is a bright scarlet with an enlarged, globular apex coloured yellow.

The fruits (follicles) are dry, boat-shaped capsules containing winged seeds from which the tree is easily propagated.

Wheel of Fire Tree is a fine, ornamental flowering tree seldom exceeding 14 m when cultivated. In its juvenile stage it can also be used as a tub house plant. The tree requires good soils in a climate with warm to hot summers, and plenty of moisture for best results. In southern Australia it is slow growing, but permanent, and is a most distinctive addition to any garden.

SCRUB BEEFWOOD *S. salignus* R. Br. is a common rainforest tree of mainly New South Wales, where it reaches nearly 33 m. In cultivation it is only a small, densely branched tree, requiring similar conditions to the Wheel of Fire Tree. The leaves are narrowly elliptical with three prominent longitudinal (or striate) nerves. Flowers are white in attractive small rosettes, and fruits are long bean-like follicles. The timber is considered very ornamental.

S. salignus

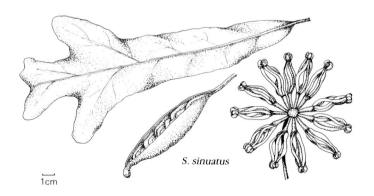

S. sinuatus

1cm

TURPENTINE TREE

Syncarpia glomulifera (Smith) Niedenzu
(syn. *S. laurifolia* Ten.)
MYRTACEAE

There are two Australian species of the genus *Syncarpia*, and they are known as turpentines. The name is derived from the orange-red resin which resembles turpentine, and protects the timber from termites and borers.

S. glomulifera is a towering shaft-like timber tree, usually 30–70 m high. A species abundant in the eastern coastal scrub forests of Queensland and New South Wales, it prefers deep fertile soils in valleys and depressions, although it is found in many other soils and situations in these areas.

It is a handsome, upright, somewhat conical tree, particularly when young, with a thick, fibrous, stringy, persistent brown bark. Leaves are oval-oblong, 5–9 cm long, opposite, and dark green with dense woolly whitish hairs on the underside. The creamy flowers, which appear in spring, are in dense, globular heads on stout stalks and are much loved by bees. Fruits consist of three-celled capsules united into a small head and containing numerous tiny seeds.

Timber of the turpentines is particularly valuable for its durability both in exposed situations and in sea-water construction, as it is resistant to marine borers. It is a dark pinkish brown in colour, hard, tough, and heavy, with many uses besides those mentioned.

FRASER ISLAND TURPENTINE *S. hillii* Bailey, also known as Peebeen, is native to Fraser Island off the Queensland coast. It has longer leaves than the preceding species, up to 12 cm long, but is very similar in general appearance.

A closely related genus, *Choricarpia*, which is distinguished by its more or less free fruits, includes two species once listed under *Syncarpia*.

BRUSH TURPENTINE *C. leptopetala* (F. Muell.) Domin. is a much smaller tree of the eastern scrub forests, seldom exceeding about 16 m in height. The wavy leaves are yellowish green in colour, giving the tree an attractive overall effect. Flowering when very young, it forms a useful street tree for subtropical regions. It is widely distributed from Brisbane to south of Sydney.

GIANT IRONWOOD *C. subargentea* (C. T. White) L. Johnson is a tall, shaft-like forest tree from south-east Queensland only, with a thin, smooth bark.

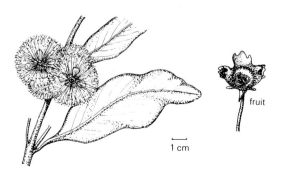

fruit

1 cm

BRUSH CHERRY

Syzygium paniculatum Gaertn.
MYRTACEAE

Often called lilly pillies, the syzygiums and the closely related acmenas (or eugenias) are, as a group, perhaps the most frequently cultivated of all Australia's rainforest trees. Although of varying habit, they are all shapely, dense evergreen trees with glossy leaves, and usually colourful, attractive fruits.

Brush Cherry is probably the hardiest species of the genus, and is often seen in gardens. It is found naturally in the brush forests from Illawarra to Atherton, often hanging over streams, and has been called Creek Lilly Pilly. Under these conditions the tree is often irregular in growth, but in cultivation it is an upright, symmetrical tree, 10–16 m high, with dark, scaly bark, and of very handsome appearance. Leaves, in opposite pairs, are glossy, lanceolate and 5–8 cm long. New shoots are reddish and shiny, and add to the tree's attraction. The fluffy, cream-coloured flowers are borne in abundant and attractive panicles in November–December but the fruits which appear in late summer and autumn provide the main display. These are bright purplish red, oval, and variable in size, occurring in dense, cherry-like bunches. Each fruit contains a solitary seed surrounded by fleshy pulp which is succulent and edible, but not particularly tasty, being rather acid in flavour. A well-formed tree loaded down by these coloured fruits is a very handsome sight.

LILLY PILLY *Acmena smithii* (Poir.) Merr. & Perry is a very similar tree found in rainforests from Victoria to Cape York Peninsula, and in the Northern Territory. The flowers are less conspicuous, and fruits are smaller and globular to elliptic, usually a pinkish colour. This species is also extensively cultivated. Several other cultivated species, all native to the east coast, are: RED APPLE *A. australis* (C. Moore.) L. Johnson, a tall handsome tree with showy masses of light red fruits; SMALL-LEAVED WATER GUM *S. luehmannii* L. Johnson, a large densely foliaged tree with reddish, pear-shaped fruits; WEEPING MYRTLE *S. floribundum* F. Muell., a large, thick-trunked tree with rough fissured bark and somewhat drooping foliage; BLUE-FRUITED LILLY PILLY *S. coolminianum* Johnson, only a small tree with numerous, bluish, urn-shaped fruits which make a fine display.

Syzygiums and acmenas are usually quick growing, and require non-limy, moist soils for best results.

1 cm

Acmena smithii

1 cm

Syzygium paniculatum

TREE WARATAH, GIPPSLAND WARATAH

Telopea oreades F. Muell.
PROTEACEAE

The waratahs are one of Australia's most famous wildflowers. The name is derived from *telopas*, meaning distance, referring to the great distance from which the flowers are visible. Tree Waratah is native to East Gippsland in Victoria and to the south-east coast of New South Wales, where it grows to a small, shapely tree 10–14 m high at its best. It favours well-drained soils in sheltered places with an annual rainfall exceeding 750 mm.

It has a thin, smooth, dark brown bark on a trunk never more than 50 cm in diameter. The smooth, dark green, lanceolate leaves, 10–20 cm long, are rather thick, narrowed at the base, and often with recurved margins. Although not as large as those of the famous New South Wales Waratah, the unusual dark red flowers are showy, appearing in terminal clusters which collectively look like a large rounded flower about 10 cm in diameter. It blooms in summer.

Often found lining the banks of streams, the tree can then be viewed from nearby hillsides. The masses of red flowers are a delight in springtime.

Fruits are curved, leathery follicles, and the timber is light brown with an attractive grain.

T. mongaensis Cheel, from southern New South Wales, is very similar, and the genus contains two further species.

TASMANIAN WARATAH *T. truncata* R. Br. is a small erect or spreading tree or shrub, up to 8 m high, but usually less, common in the mountain ranges of Tasmania. The leaves, which are 5–12 cm long, are smaller than those of Tree Waratah but otherwise it is similar to that species. It flowers in December, and has a yellow flowering form as well as the usual red.

NEW SOUTH WALES WARATAH *T. speciosissima* R. Br. is the best-known species, being extensively cultivated for cut flowers where conditions are suitable. It is usually a tall, slender, rather stiff shrub with handsome leathery, lobed leaves, and magnificent heads of large, crimson flowers which last for weeks when cut. It is a common plant in the Blue Mountains near Sydney and is the floral emblem of New South Wales. This shrub flowers in late spring to summer.

All the waratahs dislike lime or alkaline soils, and seem to grow best in rather poor, stony, well-drained soils.

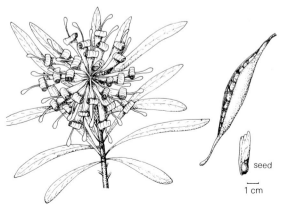

seed

1 cm

A SEA ALMOND

Terminalia muelleri Benth.
COMBRETACEAE

Terminalia trees come from areas of high summer rainfall. The genus has about 250 species spread across the tropical countries of the world, 29 of these being native to Australia.

Terminalia muelleri favours sunny areas on the edge of coastal rainforest and is often found growing near the sea behind the frontal sand dune species. It may be found from near Rockhampton north to the Gulf of Carpentaria.

The name *Terminalia* is derived from the Latin *terminus* (end), referring to the tree's habit of bearing leaves at the end of the twigs. *T. muelleri* is no exception in this regard and displays a broad canopy of leafy branches which give good shade. It is only a smallish tree 6–8 m high normally, but grows much taller in mountain forests. Bark is dark grey and rough, and the leaves are glabrous, obovate, usually 8–10 cm long by 4–6 cm wide, and prominently veined. Young buds may be silky-hairy.

The small, whitish, mainly bisexual flowers occur in loose spikes about September. Fruits are almond-shaped, 2–2·5 cm long, blue, and rather acid to the taste.

This is a monsoonal tree which deciduates in spring but is rarely totally without leaves. It grows happily to the beach foreshore, where it forms a useful shade tree for most of the year.

DAMSON *T. sericocarpa* F. Muell. is a taller tree to 30 m high which is widely distributed from about the Rockhampton area north to Cape York and across the 'Top End' to the Kimberleys. It features fruits and seeds which are edible and have a delicious flavour. The fruits are coated with silky hairs.

INDIAN or SEA ALMOND *T. catappa* L., with its horizontal branches arranged in tiers and large leaves, giving dense shade, is perhaps the most common *Terminalia* tree of the tropical shoreline of northern Australia, where it is prominent along the popular beaches in the Cairns district. This species, however, is most likely a naturalised escape plant from the tropical islands to the north of Australia.

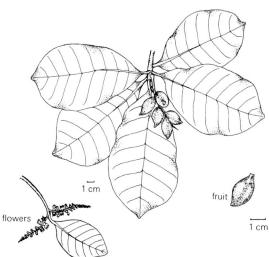

flowers

1 cm

fruit

1 cm

RED CEDAR

Toona australis (F. Muell.) Harms.
(syn. *Cedrela toona* Roxb. ex Rottler
var. *australis* (F. Muell.) C. DC.)
MELIACEAE

Red Cedar is a giant, handsome deciduous tree, native to the rainforests of the east coast, from south of Sydney to Cape York Peninsula in northern Queensland. Once the pride of the Queensland rainforests and much sought after for its fragrant, soft, highly figured timber, the tree has now become rare and is seldom seen growing naturally, except perhaps in inaccessible country. The early colonists opened up many new areas in search of this tree, and unfortunately almost eliminated one of these forests' finest assets.

Red Cedar is closely related to the Indian Toona Tree. It is known to reach heights of 70 m with a trunk 3 m in diameter, well buttressed at the base. Bark is brown or grey and scaly, and is shed in fibrous flakes leaving a smooth, reddish trunk beneath. Although tall and upright, the tree is well branched with a shapely, medium-sized crown. The handsome, pinnate leaves are alternate, and consist of 3–8 pairs of leaflets, each leaflet 4–10 cm in length, and converging to a long point at the apex. Flowers are small and sweetly perfumed, blooming in spring in large panicles at the ends of the branchlets, and are white or pale pink in colour. The fruit is a dry, oval capsule, about 2·5 cm long, five-valved, and containing long winged seeds.

The timber of the Red Cedar is soft, light, and durable, beautifully figured, and much valued for ornamental woodwork, furniture, and other uses. It polishes to a rich red colour which is enhanced as it ages.

This tree is occasionally cultivated in parks and large gardens, where it forms a large, shapely tree usually exceeding 33 m in height. It grows rapidly when planted in the tropics, but is often retarded by attacks from the Red Cedar Tip Moth. The tree is quite successful as far south as Adelaide, but prefers deep, rich soils and abundant water.

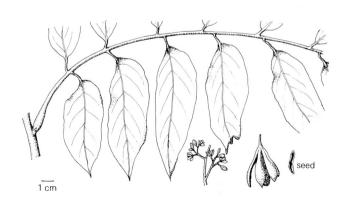

1 cm

seed

Acknowledgments

Apart from the late Ron Hill, whose sketches are gratefully acknowledged in the Introduction, special thanks go to Rob Swinbourne of the Technical Advisory Service of the Adelaide Botanic Gardens, and to Tony Irvine of the Tropical Forest Research Centre of CSIRO, for their assistance with a number of technical enquiries.

Photographic acknowledgement is accorded the following persons, some of whom assisted with photographs that were not finally used.

R. N. Auchterlonie (*Telopea oreades*)

Ian Bond (*Adansonia gregorii*)

John Brock (*Peltophorum pterocarpum*)

Brian Crafter (*Eucalyptus salmonophloia*)

Laurie Crooks (*Hakea suberea*)

the late Ron Hill (*Acacia cambagei, Araucaria bidwillii, Ceratopetalum apetalum, Kingia australis, Livistona mariae*)

David Hockings, Society for Growing Australian Plants, Brisbane

Darryl Krahenbuehl (*Acacia estrophiolata*)

Ross McKinnon and Malcolm Cox, Mount Coot-tha Botanic Gardens, Brisbane (*Barklya syringifolia, Buckinghamia celsissima, Euodia elleryana* [close-up only])

R. S. Shinkfield (*Eucalyptus papuana*)

Roger Walker (*Angophora costata*)

Geoffrey Watton (*Eucalyptus erythrocorys, E. largiflorens, E. salubris, Nuytsia floribunda*)

Bibliography

ANDERSON, R. H., *Trees of New South Wales* (Government Printer, Sydney, 4th edn 1968).

Australian Plants, Journal of the Society for Growing Australian Plants, various issues.

AUSTRALIAN SYSTEMATIC BOTANIC SOCIETY (J. Jessop, editor-in-chief), *Flora of Central Australia* (Reed, Sydney, 1981).

BEADLE, N. C. W., EVANS, O. D. & CAROLIN, R. C., *Flora of the Sydney Region* (Reed, Sydney, 1973).

BLACK, J. M., *Flora of South Australia*, 2nd edn (Government Printer, Adelaide, 1943–57).

BOLAND, D. J., BROOKER, M. I. H., CHIPPENDALE, G. N., HALL, N., HYLAND, B. P. M., JOHNSTON, R. D., KLEINIG, D. A. & TURNER,

J. D., *Forest Trees of Australia* (Nelson–CSIRO, Melbourne, 1984).

BOOMSMA, C. D., *Native Trees of South Australia* (Woods and Forests Department of South Australia, Bulletin No. 19) (Government Printer, Adelaide, 1972).

CHIPPENDALE, G. M., *Eucalyptus Buds and Fruits* (Forestry and Timber Bureau, Canberra, 1968).

CHIPPENDALE, G. M., *Eucalypts of the Western Australian Goldfields (and the Adjacent Wheatbelt)* (Australian Government Publishing Service, Canberra, 1973).

COSTERMANS, L. F., *Native Trees of South Eastern Australia* (Rigby, Adelaide, 1981).

ELLIOT, W. RODGER & JONES, DAVID L., *Encyclopaedia of Australian Plants Suitable for Cultivation*, vols 2 and 3 (Lothian, Melbourne, 1982 and 1984).

FRANCIS, W. D., *Australian Rain Forest Trees* (Australian Government Publishing Service, Canberra, 4th edn 1981).

GARDNER, C. A., *Trees of Western Australia* (Department of Agriculture of Western Australia, various Bulletins), reprinted from the *Journal of Agriculture of Western Australia*, 1952–63.

GEORGE, A. S., *The Banksia Book* (Kangaroo Press in association with the Society for Growing Australian Plants [New South Wales], Sydney, 1984).

HARMER, JENNY, *Northern Australian Plants, Part I: Top End Wildflowers* (Society for Growing Australian Plants, Sydney, 1983).

HARRIS, THISTLE Y., *Australian Plants for the Garden* (Angus & Robertson, Sydney, 1953).

HEARNE, D. A., *Trees of Darwin and Northern Australia* (Australian Government Publishing Service, Canberra, 1975).

HOCKINGS, F. D. & DANIELS, C. A., *The Australian Gardener's Guide to Flowering Trees* (Reed, Sydney, 1981).

HOLLIDAY, IVAN & LOTHIAN, NOEL, *Growing Australian Plants*, 2nd edn (Rigby, Adelaide, 1974).

HOLLIDAY, IVAN & WATTON, GEOFFREY, *A Field Guide to Banksias* (Rigby, Adelaide, 1975).

HOLLIDAY, IVAN & WATTON, GEOFFREY, *A Gardener's Guide to Eucalypts* (Rigby, Adelaide, 1980).

JESSOP, J. P., *A List of the Vascular Plants of South Australia* (State Herbarium of South Australia, Adelaide, 2nd edn 1984).

JOHNSON, L. A. S., Notes on Casuarinaceae II, *Journal of Adelaide Botanic Gardens* 6(1): 73–87 (1982).

KELLY, STAN, *Eucalypts*, vol. 1 (Thomas Nelson, Melbourne, 1969).

KELLY, S., CHIPPENDALE, G. M. & JOHNSTON, R. D., *Eucalypts*, vol. 2 (Thomas Nelson, Melbourne, 1978).

MAIDEN, J. H., *The Forest Flora of New South Wales*, vols 1–8 (Government Printer, Sydney, 1904–25).

OAKMAN, H., *Some Trees of Australia* (Jacaranda, Brisbane, 1962).

SOCIETY FOR GROWING AUSTRALIAN PLANTS, Queensland Region, *A Horticultural Guide to Australian Plants*, set 7 (Society for Growing Australian Plants, Brisbane, 1980).

STANLEY, T. D. & ROSS, E. M., *Flora of South East Queensland*, vol. 1 (Queensland Department of Primary Industries, Miscellaneous Publication 81020, Brisbane, 1983).

WHIBLEY, D. J. E., *Acacias of South Australia* (Government Printer, Adelaide, 1980).

WILLIAMS, KEITH A. W., *Native Plants of Queensland*, vols 1 and 2 (Williams, Brisbane, 1979 and 1984).

WILLIS, J. H., *A Handbook to Plants in Victoria*, vol. 2 (Melbourne University Press, Melbourne, 1972).

Glossary

adpressed or appressed: Pressed close to, or lying flat against something — e.g. referring to the hairs on a leaf.

alternate: Placed at different levels — referring to the position of successive leaves on the branchlets.

anther: The pollen-bearing part of a stamen.

aril: An expansion of the basal stalk of a seed (or ovule) into a fleshy appendage.

axil: The angle between a part and its parent body — e.g. a leaf and the main stem of a plant.

bipinnate: Of leaves, pinnate and with the leaflets again divided into secondary leaflets — e.g. the leaves of many species of *Acacia*.

bracteole: A small bract immediately below the calyx of a flower.

calcareous: Referring to a soil, of limestone origin.

calyx: The whorl of perianth parts below the corolla; collective term for the sepals.

capitate: Forming a rounded head.

capsule: A dry fruit formed from a multi-carpelled ovary.

carpel: The female part of a flower, which bears the ovules — one or more carpels comprise the ovary.

catkin: A spike formed from a pendulous rachis (primary axis) bearing unisexual flowers.

cladode: A leaf-like stem functioning as a true leaf.

corymb: An inflorescence with flowers approximately at one level due to varying pedicel lengths. The lowermost or outside flowers, which open first, have longer pedicels than the upper ones.

cotyledon: Primary leaf developed in a seed; seed leaf.

cyme: A broad, rather flat-topped inflorescence with the first-formed flower in the centre opening first. Subsequent flowers are produced by growth from a lateral bud.

deciduate: To shed leaves, bark, etc. at the end of the growing season.

deciduous: Shedding leaves or bark at the end of the growing season.

decorticate: To shed bark.

decussate: Arranged in opposite pairs, each pair at right angles to its following pair — referring to the leaf arrangement on a stem.

disc: A small development of the receptacle around the ovary.

drupe: A succulent fruit with a hard stone enclosing a single seed.

elliptical: Oval and symmetrical.

endemic: Confined to a particular country or region.

endocarp: The stone surrounding a kernel or seed; the inner wall of a pericarp or drupe — the pericarp being the fleshy fruit or wall surrounding the endocarp.

entire: Without toothing or divisions — referring to the leaves.

epiphyte: A plant growing on a host plant with no connection to the soil, and depending on decayed matter from the host for its nutrients.

falcate: Sickle-shaped; flat, curving, and tapering to a point.

fastigiate: Conical or pyramid-shaped and with close, erect branches.

filament: The stalk of an anther.

fissure: Narrow cleft or opening (in the bark of a tree).

flexuous: Zigzag.

follicle: A dry fruit containing more than one seed and splitting open along one side only — e.g. the fruit of *Grevillea*.

funicle: The basal stalk of an ovule or seed.

glabrous: Without hairs, smooth.

glaucous: Covered with a whitish or bluish bloom or powder, often giving an ashy or blue-green effect.

hoary: Covered with short, dense whitish or pale grey hairs.

hypanthium: A floral cup or tube.

imbricate: Overlapping.

included: Not projecting.

inflorescence: The flower-bearing system.

lanceolate: Lance-shaped, widest below the middle and tapered to the apex, the length at least three times the width.

lateritic: Of soil, containing laterite or ironstone.

leaflet: The ultimate segment of a compound leaf.

lenticel: Space or pore in the outer bark of most plants.

linear: Long and narrow with more or less parallel sides.

lobe: Rounded segment of a structure — e.g. some leaves are divided into several lobes.

Malesia: Floral region including Malaysia, Indonesia and the Philippines.

midrib: The main central vein of a leaf, when raised.

mucro: A sharp terminal point.

nerve: *See* vein.

node: The region of the stem from which a leaf or root arises.

obovate: Reversed ovate; egg-shaped with narrow end attached to stalk.

operculum: A cap or lid (covering the flowers of *Eucalyptus*).

opposite: At the same level but on opposite sides of a node — referring to the leaf arrangement on a branchlet.

ovary: The part of the flower which contains the ovules.

ovate: Egg-shaped and broadest below the middle.

ovule: The site of egg-cell or seed formation in a plant; the young seed in the ovary prior to fertilisation.

palmate: Arranged in a fan-shaped formation.

panicle: A branched cluster of flowers with pedicels or stalks.

pedicel: The stalk of an individual flower.

peduncle: The stalk of a cluster of flowers, or of an individual flower if this is the only member of the inflorescence.

pedunculate: Having a peduncle; being attached by a peduncle.

perianth: The collective term for the calyx and corolla of a flower, particularly applicable to many Proteaceae flowers.

petiole: The stalk of a leaf.

phyllode: A flattened leaf stalk or petiole which functions as a leaf.

pinnae: The main divisions or leaflets of a pinnate leaf.

pinnate: With leaflets arranged on both sides of a central stalk (rachis) in feather-like fashion.

pollard: To cut off or prune the whole crown of a tree.

pubescent: Covered with short, soft hairs or down.

pungent: Terminating in a stiff, sharp point.

pyramidal: Pyramid- or cone-shaped.

raceme: A simple inflorescence with a central axis producing stalked flowers along its length, the oldest ones being at the base.

rachis: The primary axis of an inflorescence or a compound leaf.

receptacle: Tip of a floral stem; the part of the stem immediately below the flower.

recurved: Curving backwards.

reflexed: Bent or turned sharply backwards.

rhomboid or rhombic: Rhomboid-shaped, diamond-shaped.

scabrous: Rough to touch.

sclerophyll forest: A forest dominated by evergreen sclerophyllous trees (trees with hard-textured leaves such as *Eucalyptus*).

serrated: With saw-toothed edges or margins.

sessile: Without a stalk.

spike: A raceme of sessile flowers.

stamen: Male part of a flower, consisting of a filament (stalk) and a pollen-bearing anther.

stigma: The part of a carpel which receives the pollen.

stipule: A lateral lobe of a leaf borne near or at the base of the petiole.

striate: Having fine longitudinal lines (striae) — e.g. describing the venation of some leaves.

style: The sterile part of a carpel connecting a stigma to its ovary.

terete: Needle-like; shaped like a narrow tapered shaft.

terminal: At the tip or end.

testa: Seed coat.

tomentum: A mat or covering of dense, woolly hairs.

trifoliolate: Term describing a compound leaf which bears three leaflets.

umbel: An arrangement of pedicellate flowers arising from a common point of the floral axis or peduncle.

umbrageous: Providing shade.

undulate: Rippled — esp. referring to leaf margin.

unisexual: Of one sex — e.g. a flower where only one sex is present.

valve: One segment of a fruit which naturally splits open at maturity, usually containing seeds.

vein: Strand of conducting tissue in a leaf.

venation: The pattern of vein arrangement.

viable: Capable of development — referring to the germination of seeds.

villous: Covered with long soft hairs.

whorl: Group of organs arranged in radial fashion around an axis — e.g. a radial group of leaves or flowers at a node.

Index of Common Names

Index of Scientific Names
Names not in italics are synonyms.